DO YOU SAY "SIR"
TO YOUR FATHER?

All the best !

Brian Denoon

DO YOU SAY "SIR"
TO YOUR FATHER?

TALES AND MEMORIES OF THE GREAT GLEN

BY

BRIAN DENOON

ILLUSTRATIONS AND COVER DESIGN BY NIALL MACLENNAN

ARDVRECK PUBLISHING

4

Published in **Inverness** in 2009 by

Ardvreck Publishing

13 Lombard Street,

Inverness

IV1 1QQ

ISBN 979-0-9561845-0-4

A CIP Catalogue record for this book is

available from the British Library

Printed by ForTheRightReasons Community Print

5

Contents

Foreword   9

Chapter 1   Great Glen Memories – Introduction   11

Chapter 2   The Abriachan Years   15

Chapter 3   War Clouds over Abriachan   19

Chapter 4   The Abriachan Blitz and the Eye of Satan   23

Chapter 5   Behind the Façade.   28

Chapter 6   Fort Augustus   33

Chapter 7   The Parrot from Hell and The Village Hall   37

Chapter 8   The Local Grocery Tycoon   43

Chapter 9   Shinty – and the Lay Preacher   49

Chapter 10 The Fort Scout Troop   55

Chapter 11   Primary Care   59

Chapter 12 Go East, Young Man   69

Chapter 13 In the Shadow of the Gasworks   78

Chapter 14 The Bridge Street Bogey Man   83

Chapter 15 Fred J Kelly's   86

Chapter 16 Nicked   89

Chapter 17 The Glenurquhart experience   92

Chapter 18 Bus People and the Homework Blight   97

Chapter 19 Epic Belting of Fifty Two   103

Chapter 20 Clash of Cultures   109

Chapter 21 Victoria Buildings   113

Chapter 22 The Labourer – and the Worthiness

of his Hire - Forestry Days   120

Chapter 23 Mystery in the Elite Squad   130

Chapter 24 In the Dry Canteen   134

Chapter 25 Placating the Captain   143

Chapter 26 Village Dances   154

Chapter 27 Vehicles I Have Known BCX 909   166

Chapter 28 HUY 807   171

Chapter 29 KST 486   176

Chapter 30 Jeep   184

Chapter 31 Son of Albion   189

Chapter 32 Bob Miller's Mill   195

Chapter 33 Perkeo 1   199

Chapter 34 Little Did We Know   204

FOR SHEILA AND CATRIONA

Foreword

It is not unusual for an author to request from a fellow writer a few paragraphs to be placed before his text as a recommendation to read on. In this case the normal pattern of events was reversed. Having heard that **Brian Denoon** was intending to print his experiences of growing up in the Great Glen for posterity, I insisted that he permit me to provide him with a Foreword to his book.

Why so? Principally because as Editor of the *Glenurquhart Bulletin* since 1999 I have had the privilege of receiving from Brian on annual basis one of a series of articles describing aspects of his upbringing and schooling on Loch Ness-side. These pieces were individually and collectively memorable. Beautifully crafted, illustrated with acutely observed detail of period and personality, they soon became required reading for the folk of the Glen, at home and abroad.

Now these pieces – and much more besides - have been gathered together and, aided by the sympathetic illustrations of artist **Niall Maclennan**, have found a lasting home under the title **"Do you say 'Sir' to your father?"**

Of course memoirs about growing up in a Highland glen exist in profusion in the literature of the North. However, Brian Denoon's memories of the Great Glen in the immediate post war years have a unique appeal. For one thing he writes about the period encompassed by the dates 1946-1960. This was a time which saw the traditional way of life in the north undergo massive and permanent changes. First electricity, then television came to the Great Glen. It was also the era of huge hydro schemes, road improvements and the erosion of a traditional way of life linked to forestry, crofting and seasonal work on sporting estates.

These topics, and more, grace the following pages - but what makes them a marvellous read is the exceptional quality of the writing. Simply put, Brian is a stylist with a passion for language and, truth to tell, few are better qualified than he is to write about the Great Glen - in particular, that part of it which lies between Fort Augustus and the Highland capital, Inverness.

Brought up in Abriachan and Fort Augustus where his Glen Urquhart - born father was headmaster, Brian was educated at Glen Urquhart Senior Secondary School and Aberdeen University. In his youth he played shinty for both the Glen Urquhart school team and Aberdeen University from where he graduated to a lifetime of teaching first at Inverness High School and then as Principal Teacher of English, at Charleston Academy, Inverness. An experienced freelance journalist and former broadcaster at *BBC Highland*, he was for a time the shinty correspondent for *The Scotsman.*

I certainly did not call my father "Sir": neither did Brian. But the very fact that in recent memory there could exist a race living in the Highlands who actually did so, is only one of the many attractions of this eminently readable book.

Fraser Mackenzie

Great Glen Memories

This book was meant to be exclusively about the Nineteen Fifties – perhaps easing over into the very early appearance of the Sixties. Actually it will start by looking back into the Forties.

All this will make sense presently. It is mainly, however, about the Nineteen Fifties in the Great Glen in the Highlands of Scotland. It is how I saw and remember them during school and university days. A structured social history of that decade it most definitely is not.

And who am I? Well, I spent the major part of my life trying to teach English to the young of Inverness and hinterland. I was born and brought up in the Great Glen – or that part of it that lies between Fort Augustus, at the centre, and the Highland capital, Inverness. School first in Abriachan then in Fort Augustus where I was taught by both parents; later in Glenurquhart where the headmaster was a second cousin on my father's, and also an inglorious spell in Inverness Royal Academy where I wasn't related to any of the teachers. Then on to Aberdeen University to gain that uniquely Scottish qualification, the Ordinary MA, with its marvellous mixture of English Literature: Ordinary and Advanced, French, History, Moral Philosophy and one Science subject – Geology in my case. As well as being able to quote bits of the classics at you, I can still identify Boddam Porphyry and Mica Schist. A grateful beneficiary of the ethos of the Democratic Intellect. After gaining my teaching qualifications – also in Aberdeen – it was back to the Great Glen. It never occurred to me to head elsewhere. My working life as a teacher was spent in Inverness High School (until 1978) and then in Charleston Academy. It was from this latter that I gained my freedom in 1988 with (blessed) early retirement.

As far as decades go, The Nineteen Fifties surely have to be the most grey and non-descript of all such decimal groupings of the years of the twentieth century. It is a decade that came into being when all were exhausted after the vast upheavals of the World War. It preceded the explosion of self-expression, libertarianism and sexual licence that we are all told took place in the Nineteen Sixties. The Sixties together with the Seventies, the Eighties and the Nineties all have their stamps and identity tags affixed to them associating them with varying degrees of outrageous human behaviour. But the

Fifties? Post-War austerity meant that they didn't even have universally available colour photography to record them. Images from that time are consequently grey, dark and unrelievedly gloomy. Clothing was drab, and styles for both genders were dull and crushingly unimaginative. Square box-like outlines for the males and long skirts and cardigans for the girls. Only the pronounced conical bras that made their appearance then – to loud choruses of disapproval – were able to raise a frisson. Girls' hair was compacted and primped close to the skull, while boys smeared the oily contents of Brylcreem jars on to their hair, to help to flatten it down on either side of long, white partings. Yet, while we were living through it, it was obviously all that we could know. There were some contrasts with the decades of our parents' generation, but they were not all that dramatic. I suppose this era is best summed up for me in sartorial terms. It was the raincoats so many of us wore then. They were identical to the kind that KGB operatives and spies wore in films – double-breasted, square-shouldered, grey, belted and made of gabardine. They were a cut-down version of what the older generation wore. There was no allowance for anything like a youth culture in such matters in those days. Originally I thought that I would call this collection "Great Glen Tales", but the realisation that it contained an unplanned and all too obvious pun had me change my mind. Instead, so strong is my recollection of these grim garments that I then decided to call this collection "The Gabardine Years". But then a third impression overtook these and made the title something quite different. Bear with me.

The Fifties was assuredly a decade that style had passed by. In case you might wonder that I have not mentioned the Teddy Boy style of the fifties that had the older generation in apoplexy – well, it just didn't really penetrate into the Highland village I lived in then. I only came into contact with it when I went to university in Aberdeen in 1956. Even then, it was something utterly strange and, I have to say, decidedly not for me. Not a moral objection – just not my style.

My earliest memories come from the War years in that tiny scattering of houses called Abriachan, high in the hills above Loch Ness, about ten miles from Inverness, where my father was headmaster from 1935 until 1944. From there, we went to Fort Augustus, where my father and mother both retired from teaching in 1971. Also included are Glenurquhart, (where I received much of my later schooling), Glenmoriston and Inverness.

In spite of my totally negative comments on the Fifties so far, there were positive aspects as well. First of all, consider the coming of the Hydro Electric schemes. The huge impact made by these cannot be exaggerated. My home village of Fort Augustus didn't have a generating station or a dam built nearby, but in Invergarry to the west and Glen Moriston to the east, huge engineering works were under way in the Fifties. Hundreds of men flooded in to work on these dams and to tunnel through the hills. They were accommodated in enormous, primitive camps specially built for them. These men had a profound impact on Highland life. For a start, the wages they earned were quite startlingly higher than you would expect from employers like the Forestry Commission. Many local men and women got jobs with "the Hydro". Then there was the occasion when Loch Ness was visited briefly and tragically by the cutting edge of jet power technology, when the ill-fated world water speed record attempt failed so spectacularly before the lenses of the world's press in September 1952. John Cobb's graceful speedboat, "Crusader" disintegrated at around 230 miles per hour, and he was hurled to his very public death. Significantly I also remember that day as an example of the unthinking barbarity of school discipline as it was practised in those days.

Then there was much to take up our energies and imaginations – not least the myriad of casual jobs that were freely available for school pupils and students then and which provided the money for the awakening appetites. Some of the attitudes of those days seem now to come from a distant planet. There was the absurd class system, illustrated in the chapter entitled "Placating the Captain". It was from this episode that I have taken the final title for my reminiscences.

So, the things that are the landmarks of my Great Glen Tales: Abriachan in the war years, secondary education in two very different schools, the marvellous variety and excitement of the casual jobs that I did as a school pupil and as a university student. I didn't receive a student grant while attending Aberdeen University, so these jobs were vital to me, if only to salve my conscience in my awareness that my parents (both being teachers) had to support me. These jobs gave me a sense of adventure and excitement and the education in life they afforded me was huge, packed as it was into a modest number of years. (I had missed National Service by a whisker: late acceptance by the university had seen me go though all the business of selection for the army.)

It is in that area that most of the tales in this collection are set.

Some of the chapters are versions of articles that were originally published in the Inverness Courier, while a few others appeared in the Glenurquhart Bulletin. The rest have been based on radio programmes broadcast on the BBC or have been written for this book.

Brian Denoon
March 2009

The Abriachan Years

My father, Robert Andrew Denoon, became the head teacher in the school in Abriachan in 1935. Before that, he had been headmaster in Elgol on the Island of Skye. It was one of the appointments that marked the continuation of the era of anti Gaelic policies throughout the Highlands in those days. My father, although his mother was a fluent Gaelic speaker, had never learned the language more than the occasional word or expression. Yet, when the authorities looked for a suitable young man to take over the small school down by the shores of Loch Scavaig, and where Gaelic was the predominant language then, it was natural that they would choose a non-Gaelic speaker such as my father. He spent several very happy years there, but when the call of the mainland came, it was to Abriachan he went in 1935, with his new wife, Robina MacPhee, also a teacher, to settle in the schoolhouse in the fold of the hills, high above Loch Ness. In 1935, Abriachan was a scattered but identifiable Highland community. Its main focal points were the school and the nearby tiny village hall. There was not even a church. The minister from Lochend (down at the east end of Loch Ness) would take services in the hall. There was no shop either, but there was a Post Office. Abriachan today is still identifiable as a community, but few – if any - of the present inhabitants in their recently built homes have any connection with the original people of the village.

My father was to be the headmaster there throughout most of the war years and although I was very young, I have been left with powerful impressions and memories of these days. Many are actual memories – much of the rest is what I have subsequently heard and assimilated from my parents. There are the various extraordinary Abriachan characters who still live on in my memory and whose eccentricities and odd - even bizarre – behaviour have taken firm shape in my imagination as if I had actually known them myself. Of course, some of them I actually do remember from first hand. There were John and Mrs Finlay (pronounced "Finla"; and always ""Mrs". Her first name was never used, although she was always a close and supportive friend to our family.) They lived close by, in a croft, Leult, – their small white house right beside the bridge over the burn. Her small husband I can only see as a pipe-smoking kindly presence, sitting by the kitchen window during one of our many visits. There was Johndo. He was the simpleton odd-job man who stayed at the croft with the Finlays. He always seemed to be at our back door, asking my father for some tobacco for his pipe. Silly Willie Brodie was a tramp who called at sort of regular times for something to eat and a cup of tea. The "Silly" was his own addition to his name, and all I remember is his beard, his dun-coloured tattered coat, and once him offering me an apple from the depths of one of its pockets. There was the "Boxer". He was called that because he played the melodeon, or box, Rod the Trapper and his wife Isa, who looked after the tiny post office. There were the Swapper, and Willie Balnagrieshashack. Then there was the gamekeeper. He was a quite alarming character. He attained some notoriety as the most unsettling member of the Abriachan platoon of the Home Guard. My father was a lieutenant in the Home Guard and the gamekeeper was probably his greatest problem – after the fear of imminent invasion. More about this man later.

The "character" syndrome of such a remote Highland community might best be illustrated by a tale, which involved Rod the Trapper and the Swapper. Both of these men had been, for a long time, as a means of earning something extra for themselves, distilling whisky in the more remote and desolate empty spaces. Rod had driven up on one occasion to see how things were progressing. Things were fine, and the two began to sample the latest batch of spirit. They fell into a deep and dreamless sleep. The Trapper awoke to a strong stench in his nostrils. He found himself surrounded by a mass of black, oily smoke. The Swapper emerged from it.

"That was a damned near thing, Rod," he announced.

"What do you mean?"

"The still had gone dry. The mash was starting to burn. The smell of the still was spreading. I've sorted it, though. There's enough smoke to cover it."

It was then that the Trapper saw what the smoke was coming from. He had driven up in his big black car that he used as a local taxi. The spare wheel, usually fixed to the back of the car, was now missing. It was lying in the centre of the fire and was completely destroyed. As far as the Swapper was concerned, the smell of burning rubber was the best way of covering up the smell of the mash that might have had their still discovered.

This was more than typical of the Swapper. His own dilapidated cottage summed him up. Somebody once asked him why he never had the hole in the roof repaired. He is said to have replied, "When it's dry, I never notice it. When it's wet, I can't do anything about it."

He seems to have had a reputation in another area also. You tampered with him at your peril. This was demonstrated when he and another local called Ally Haney quarrelled on the way back to the foot of Abriachan Brae from Inverness on MacFarlane's bus. When they got out, the Swapper forced Ally Haney down on to the pier that jutted out into Loch Ness in those days.

"Get down on your knees!" he told the wretched and by now fearful Haney. "Say your prayers. When you're done, it's into the loch for you."

Ally Haney did as he was ordered and began to stammer out his desperate prayers, sure that his time was up. Meanwhile the Swapper had tiptoed away leaving his victim in his state of terror. When my father told me this story, he was, of course, repeating what he had been told by the Swapper himself. Its veracity could never be checked.

The writer who said that the past is a foreign country did not exaggerate. My parents' arrival in the schoolhouse in Abriachan illustrates this pretty unambiguously. The house was totally uninhabitable. The wife of the previous schoolmaster had been, to put it at its most kindly, eccentric. She had a love for all living creatures; to such an extent that the house and environs were haven for the most monstrous rats, insects, spiders and whatever else that flew, crawled or scuttled about in the neighbourhood. They could all live in or near the schoolhouse completely unmolested. So far, so bad, but the real horror they were to discover was that of all the creatures she yearned to nurture, the common house cat was the obsession of her life. She had an enormous number of them and they were all kept in the front room of the schoolhouse. They were never allowed out of that room and lived out their ghastly communal lives in it. The stench has the imagination shrink from contemplation. Locals, my parents heard later, spoke of the headmaster's wife, leaving Abriachan schoolhouse for the last time. It was a day of torrential rain. She was sitting in the back of a horse-drawn cart, with her vast tribe of cats in baskets piled all around her.

No-one could inhabit that house until it had been cleared of its awful, mephitic stench – in particular, that dreadful front room. Workmen were sent. They were overwhelmed by what they found. The floorboards were ripped up and burned. The walls were stripped and re-lined. The earth in the foundations was dug out and huge quantities of powerful disinfectant were poured in. But the sheer concentration of what these cats had deposited over many years meant that the house was never to be completely free of their memory. For all of the nine years that our family lived in that house, on any still and sunny day if the windows were shut, there could still arise from some part of that room, an evil reminder of its former captive inhabitants. All this was bad enough of course, but it was the attitude of the education authorities of those days that really took some beating. During all the many months that it took to get the house habitable, the family had to stay at Drumnadrochit with our grandmother. Yet, the full rent was docked from my father's salary each month. He had been appointed to the post, and had to pay his dues. No exceptions were allowed. When he did make some complaining sounds, he was told that it was only the front room that was the problem. Technically, the rest of the house was perfectly all right. This was the decision of an official in lordly Inverness who never came to see for himself, in spite of being asked to. This arrogance was evident in another area as well. The school's supply of coal for the fireplaces in the classrooms was finished. And there were several weeks before the next lot was due to be delivered. The result of this? Well, my father, as well as having to take the bus from Drumnadrochit to the foot of the brae each morning, climbing up the formidable hill the two or so miles up to the school – as well as all of this, he carried in a knapsack, enough coal (paid for by himself of course) to start up the fires. For the rest of the fuel, he had to cut sticks from the nearby wood. As for any compensation for all of these beyond-the-call-of-duty actions – well, what do you think? Needless to say, when I was hearing about this crass behaviour by an employer, the question was, "Why on earth did you put up with this treatment?" And the answer came back: You just didn't dare to rock the boat in those days.

War Clouds over Abriachan

My father threw himself into Home Guard activities with almost daemonic energy, eventually reaching the rank of Lieutenant. As far as I was concerned, the most fascinating item of equipment he was issued with at this time was his khaki motor-bike. To be more precise, it was the domed, khaki crash helmet and the goggles that went with it. The helmet had a special leathery smell from its lining, and those goggles were like the ones that the fighter pilots wore in those days.

The TV series, "Dad's Army" has imprinted an image of the Home Guard as a doddering, well-meaning, but ultimately futile last line of defence should an invasion ever have taken place. Rather unfortunate perhaps, because it was all taken extremely seriously by the men of the Abriachan platoon. It became a quite efficient body of men and gained more than a few official accolades during various exercises – sometimes involving regular troops. It ought to be remembered as well that many of these Home Guard men were gamekeepers and men of the outdoors. Many were acquainted with firearms and were good shots as well.

Overhead, in those days, droned various aircraft – mostly ours, of course. I remember being told that the engine note of the enemy was quite different from ours, due to some basic difference in engine design. Theirs was a sinister pulsing drone. If ever there was one that sounded like that far above, then it was a headlong dash for the imagined safety of the house. Then there was that regular aerial ritual of those days (and one I have never seen referred to in any book about the war). It involved the slow, elephantine progress of a Sunderland flying boat down Loch Ness not much higher than the hills, with one or two fighters (Hurricanes or Spitfires) sweeping down in mock attacks on it. This, presumably, was to give the pilots and gunners practice for the real thing.

Abriachan was often used for practice and exercises by the regular army as well as by the Home Guard. Khaki figures were fairly often seen, with their helmets covered in netting and wrapped in their mottled gas capes if it was raining; flat, bounding bren-gun carriers seemed to float effortlessly from the road on to the heather tussocks of the moor. There would be the crackle of blank ammunition – and occasionally the real thing too. A demonstration of that crude weapon of those days – the Sten gun – almost ended rather badly for me. I had been watching (from a spot where I had no business to be – peering over the wall at the top of the garden) a group of the Home Guard. They had an instructor with them who was showing them how to use this light machine-gun. He held the weapon down low, and fired short bursts at several targets spread some yards apart. Then it was the turn of the Home Guard men. One of them seemed to panic when he pressed the trigger. He swept the muzzle past the targets in turn – but continued swinging round after he had completely missed the last one. I felt the wind of the bullets as I fell back into the raspberry bushes. I am pretty sure that I would have felt the full weight of parental retribution for this.

Not very far from where I had almost become the Home Guard's first war casualty, there stood a small window-less shed. It looked like an outside toilet in the far corner of the walled garden. But it had a more sinister purpose. It contained crates of hand-grenades and boxes of live ammunition. One day, an urgent communication came through to the effect that one consignment of Mills grenades was faulty and highly dangerous. The contents of that shed had to be closely checked for the deadly serial numbers. My father earned his pips that night as he confirmed that all these grenades were as safe as grenades ever could be.

The Abriachan platoon did not escape the fanatical demands of British Army discipline and appearance. There were inspections carried out regularly on the men and their equipment. There were visits by captains and the occasional colonel, and these kept my father very much on edge – especially when he knew full well that there were some in his platoon who were liable to bring disgrace on his head. One such was Willie Baknagrieshashack. (*This name is reproduced phonetically and from memory, I would mention here.*) He used his Home Guard issue boots all the time – strictly against regulations, and eventually they became battered and down-at-heel. One day, the platoon's boots were to be gathered to be sent into Inverness to be repaired – but before dispatch to the town, there was also to be an equipment inspection by a Captain. My father stacked up the boots so that Willie's were right at the bottom. The Captain approached and poked at the pile speculatively with his stick. The boots toppled slowly over, exposing the shameful battered remnants to the officer's ice-cold stare.

But to get back to the gamekeeper I was referring to earlier. His name was Fraser, but his nickname had a stronger almost ferocious quality to it. A forewarning of what nature of man you were dealing with. It was Polashac. He lived quite close to the school – in fact, just a few hundred yards down a track, at the foot of a damp field near the burn that flowed from Loch Laide down to Loch Ness far below. The war, to Polashac, was a total obsession. He would wear his Home Guard uniform at all times – against regulations, of course. On one occasion an army staff car drew up alongside him while he was out on the road and an officer leaned out and jabbed with his swagger stick.

"I say, there. You can't wear battledress when there hasn't been a call-out! Don't you know the regulations?"

"Aye," came the ponderously logical reply. "But do the Germans know the regulations – Sir?"

Being a gamekeeper by profession, he was naturally a good shot. But not, as it happened, the best in the platoon. Johnny Balachraggan was the one who had that honour. During practice at the range, Polashac would cause problems with his tendency to be too quick on the trigger. After his first strikes on the target had been indicated with the pointers by the concealed men in the trench below, he would open up again before they had completely got themselves safely lying down. He did this once to Johnny Balachraggan. That was enough. Later that day, it was Polashac's turn to point to the bullet holes in the targets. Scarcely had he turned away from them, when a perfectly laid pattern of bullets pierced the nearest, with attendant cracks and spurts of sand from the bank immediately behind him. My father said that he saw this actually happen. Such behaviour would normally bring down the severest of disciplinary response but it was felt that anyone who could jerk the deadly serious Polashac to his senses was to be encouraged. Even in such dangerous circumstances. Polashac was obsessed with the danger of the fifth columnists. The Nazi spies and infiltrators who were working to destroy us. He regularly patrolled Abriachan Brae to make sure that the telephone lines hadn't been cut. The interruption of such vital communications would be the first sign that Abriachan was under threat of imminent invasion, and that the parachutes would be drifting down on us all. His fanaticism in this belief reached a spectacular climax in one farcical though potentially dangerous incident. It was at a time in the hostilities where there were stories in the press about the dark treachery and satanic cunning of the Nazis. There were reports of them dropping from the skies by parachute behind allied lines – disguised as nuns or priests. One day, with his head filled with these wild tales, Polashac was out on a hillside above Loch Ness, going about his game keeping duties. As usual, he had on his complete battledress kit – helmeted and armed with his rifle. Suddenly, in the distance, he saw a figure walking along the track that led to a remote household at a place called Corriefoinas. He studied the distant figure for some time – no doubt through his telescope – and saw that he was a minister. But which minister? He wasn't the local minister whom Polashac would obviously have known. Driven by his total conviction of imminent invasion and Nazi treachery, the story was that he stalked him like a stag and at a point on the lonely road most suitable for an ambush, he sprang in front of him – a fearsome, armed, helmeted figure, with the bolt slamming home on the breech of his rifle and a live round in place. The bewildered and terrified stranger was forced to hoist his hands over his head and was submitted to a fierce grilling by a man who was convinced that he had waylaid one of the Fuhrer's roaring, blond ranks of fanatics – albeit in cunning disguise. What Polashac didn't know was that he was terrorising a visiting minister on the innocent pastoral duties of a man of the cloth. We can only guess at the agonies and terror that this wretched man went through before he managed to convince the maniacally-obsessive Polashac that he was who he said he was. Polashac was quite relaxed about it all, it seems. He had done no more nor less than any patriot would have done when his native land was under threat.

The Abriachan Blitz and the Eye of Satan

Abriachan's war continued and various shadows fell over the small community. Because of its ageing population, the chilling telegram from the War Office was not a regular event. Privations in the way of scarce commodities and reduced travel due to lack of petrol were the more daily preoccupations – apart, of course from the daily progress of the war.

And the Home Guard continued its vigilance. I make no apology for returning to this theme as it played a very large part in the life of the family at this time. My father spent an immense amount of time in the administration of the Abriachan platoon and actually taking part in field exercises of all sorts. These frequently had him away from home for many days and nights at a time. He had started out as a humble private, but finished up as Lieutenant. He might have gone even higher, but there were dark plots that conspired against him. Jealousies were virulent even in this organisation.

Bombs were even heard on two memorable occasions. Once when my father was in the Renudin Woods to the north and west of the village – over towards Kiltarlity – with his .22 rifle, looking for rabbits, he heard the drone of an aircraft. Its engine noise marked it out as German. He heard the distant thud of explosions - from the direction of Loch Ness. Shortly after, a dark, sinister shape flitted over the hills towards him and flew directly overhead with a crash of sound. Its jagged broken cross and the symbols on the undersides of its wings were clear and unambiguous. He let off a shot at it, instinctively, but with only a fleeting second of vision, there wasn't much of a chance. Not that a .22 bullet could have done much anyway by way if harm. Later it transpired that he had witnessed the enemy's attempt to destroy the aluminium factory at Foyers. The bombs had fallen wide, though one did manage to fracture a water pipe and caused flooding. As for the black raider, I have been told that he had been shot down before he made it back to his lair in distant Norway.

The other occasion when the bombs were heard in Abriachan, I can remember vaguely myself. It was night time and the terrifying, pulsing drone we associated with the enemy filled the air. The shock of the explosions seemed to be frighteningly close at hand – then we listened, rigid, to the dwindling throb of the engines. The next day revealed that eight bombs had struck a hillside above Abriachan, directly overlooking Loch Ness. They had been released, presumably, by a German crew that simply wished to dump its cargo to allow it to get back to its base more quickly. Casualties were minimal. Allie Beanlie, local talk had it, took refuge inside the chimney of his cottage while the body of a hare was picked up not far from the point of impact. A long white scar marked that hill for many years after this incident. And we still have, in our family, a shard of the shrapnel that ripped from the explosions. There is still black paint visible on one side of it.

Back to the Home Guard, though. It wasn't long before the Abriachan platoon began to get itself noticed higher up, as it were. There was the notable occasion during an exercise at Aberchalder, past Fort Augustus. There were regular troops involved in this one, and it was supervised by regular army officers and NCOs. An objective – an old mill building – was to be captured and the Abriachan platoon took it in spectacular fashion. Captain Glover, who was in overall command, looked on and was pleased.

"Congratulations, Denoon," he announced. "Yours was rated the most outstanding performance of the whole weekend."

Praise indeed. Even better, the Abriachan performance was mentioned in battalion orders the following week. A copy ought to have been sent to the Abriachan platoon, but alas – it never made its appearance. The supreme accolade never arrived. As I mentioned earlier, there appeared to be an obstacle somewhere in the chain of command that continually held back recognition of achievements or had them diverted to another place. Any deficiencies higher up, however, tended to be wrongly attributed. It was always thus in the military, and the Home Guard was no exception.

The following stories about the more farcical/dangerous side of the Home Guard have come down to me, though I cannot vouch for them having come from Abriachan. I'd like to think this first one did.

A roadblock was being manned late one evening. A well-known local drunk swayed up on his bike. The challenge was so violent that he fell from the bike, and he ended up sprawling half in and half out of the ditch. Before there was time to help him, the dim. wartime headlights of a car approached. It was the local doctor and he was in a bad mood. It was not helped by the sight of two rifles with fixed bayonets pointing straight at him.

"You know damn fine who I am," he barked when asked to identify himself.

"You don't move till we've checked," came the stolid reply.

"Look, this is arrant nonsense! Move aside, will you…"

"I wouldn't advise it." Came a cold voice from the darkness beyond the bayonet. "See what happened to the last one who tried to be funny." And the doctor's eyes were directed towards the tangled limbs of the inert drunk at the roadside.

At a similar road-block, near Inverness, a general in a staff car was signalled to stop by a Home Guard patrol. For some reason, the driver continued on his way. A shot rang out and a bullet struck the car. The driver drew to a shuddering halt. One of the Home Guard patrol leaned in and announced.

"Lucky for you you stopped. Next time I was going to aim."

I referred to the universal shortage of the basic amenities in wartime. Admittedly there were certain advantages to living in the country with the various crofts scattered around, but nevertheless, the regular visit of the grocer's van was a high spot of the week. Willie Allan's van came from Inverness and there was also Jimmy Fraser's from Kiltarlity. I have heard from my mother that Willie Allan's van called at the schoolhouse one dark and blustery evening. His usually dim interior light wasn't working – but Willie had the answer. On the counter was a candle, stuck firmly in the centre of a Burnett's mutton pie. This pie was a delicacy for generations who grew up in or near Inverness, but that sight did have a rather negative effect on my mother. She could never look at one again without seeing a wax-dripping candle sprouting from it.

My father had a tale about these days and the Spartan diet of wartime that became – with its frequent re-telling – a bit of a bore to us. Bread then was made with special government approved flour. It had the obvious basic ingredient, but there were additives to make the actual flour go further. This resulted in a dull and grey-looking plain loaf. One day, Willie Allan told my mother, conspiratorially, that he had several loaves made with pre-war quality flour. Would she like one? Well, would she! The result was so much of an experience that it was talked about again and again, with my father's final accolade for this amazing loaf rounding off the story: "It was so fine, it was like cake!" Like cake? A curious simile, but I can hear him say it yet.

Self-sufficiency was much depended upon, of course. The more obvious solution like keeping hens was helped by Mrs Finlay. She gave my mother some hens, together with a cock. All went well for a time, and the eggs duly began to make their welcome appearance. However a bizarre problem arose with the cock. It was nicknamed "Jockans" (after a famous, but harmless drunk who lived in Drumnadrochit), and it developed a profound and utterly inexplicable dislike for my mother. It would attack and try to savage her on every occasion that it could. Back to Mrs Finlay – who was very sceptical – it eventually went. His replacement was a prim and sedate creature who immediately got the nickname "Clarence". Peace again reigned in the henhouse. As for Jockans, he made the fatal error of launching an attack on the very large and robust Mrs Finlay. One blow from a broom handle had him stunned. He recovered enough to stagger at her in a last desperate kamikaze assault. This time, the broom handle dispatched Jockans for good.

My parents had been told by someone that goat's milk was especially good for rearing a robust family, so a nanny-goat appeared one day. It was kept in a wire-netting compound among apple trees at the top of the garden.

It was a truly frightful creature. I can still see it from the perspective of a seven year old, which has it loom gigantic, angular and malevolent. No need to wonder why Satan is so often depicted as a goat. The staring agate eyes - and the curved sweeping horns of the male - are the essence of the mediaeval horned devil.

And the Abriachan Goat was indeed possessed of the Devil. It did all that the perverse nature of goats drove it to do – and then more. It escaped regularly from its prison compound and destroyed vegetables and herbaceous borders. It ate the rope that tethered it. It wrestled wildly with my father with its front cloven hooves on his shoulders and its devil's eyes staring into his. All attempts to milk it were so farcical and frustrating that it was finally decided that enough was enough, and the goat had to go. There was no-one who could be persuaded to take it off our hands. My father then decided on the most drastic solution. He dug a large grave some distance beyond the school playground wall, up in the moor, and arming himself with the enormous Webley revolver that came with the rank of Lieutenant of the Home Guard, he dragged the hated beast to its place of execution.

The goat suspected something, and resisted violently. The grave yawned, and the revolver was cocked. But no shot rang out.

My father looked along the barrel and into the evil, staring eyes, but he just could not pull that trigger. The only way he could retrieve something from the situation – after he had untied the tethering rope from the goat's neck – and to release some of his own pent-up loathing was by aiming and landing a violent kick on its bony shanks. It bucked and kicked and vanished into the vast emptiness of the moor. It was never seen again, and was missed by none of us.

A final word on transport. During these war years in Abriachan, my father owned a car. And what a car! It was a model called a Triumph "Gloria". It was dark green; it had huge staring headlights and it had green leather upholstery. That's all that I can remember. You see, neither I nor any other member of the family was ever really inside it. Two reasons for this: first, the car was to be used during hostilities exclusively on Home Guard (i.e. War Office) business. Absolutely no private use was permitted. The second reason was my father's infuriating incorruptibility. Others might (and many did) have risked a small family outing some quiet afternoon, but his response was an implacable no.

So my total experience of that beautiful car consisted of waiting for it to appear over the lip of Abriachan Brae, to watching it heave itself up the last bit of the road to the school gate, and then being allowed to jump in for a run up the few yards to the garage at the top of the playground. That was my lot.

But what about after the war? All those family outings in it? Actually, he sold it before we left Abriachan in 1944. It was to be many years before our family had another car.

Behind The Façade

Abriachan was an ageing community when my parents arrived in 1935 and when my father took up his duties as the head teacher of the school there. Consequently the number of local children attending was dwindling. The actual roll of the school, however, held at around sixty five – pretty reasonable for a remote school situated high in the hills. This number was possible as a result of the number of "boarded out" children attending, who latterly made up the majority. This long-extinct term refers to an attempt in those days to try to give children from homes broken up by all kinds of social upheaval, the chance of a better life in other – presumably "normal" – homes. It is only relatively recently that I found out exactly what this term meant. I had thought that it referred exclusively to children who had been sent, like evacuees, to safety from enemy bombing in the cities. The remit was far wider than that. Since Abriachan had its aging population, there was no shortage of homes willing to take in these children. The authorities provided these foster parents with clothes and money to help to cover costs. It seems to have worked reasonably well on the whole, though it is painfully obvious that exploitation and even downright cruelty could take place. Evidence of just such cruelty came to light in a rather strange fashion in my parents' lives long after they had retired. More of this theme later.

My father found out that, although there were potential problems of discipline in a school population that contained so many children who were emotionally disturbed, he managed to get on well with them. The previous head teacher of Abriachan (the husband of the keeper of the vast tribe of cats) had his own obsession. He was a fanatical trainer of prize-winning school choirs. My father was astounded to discover that these pupils had been so thoroughly programmed that four-part harmony came to them almost instinctively. The debit side to all this was that in order to attain this degree of skill, there had been a reign of tyranny in the school. Children had had to stand for whole afternoons singing, until some even fainted. Others would get belted for not performing to their full capacity. Needless to say all of this was at the expense of normal school subjects. However from this unnatural crucible, came two national awards in successive years – a coveted shield. The Abriachan School Choir was poised to lift it for a third time, when against the popular feeling of the audience present at the adjudication, the prize went elsewhere. It was said that the great Sir Hugh Roberton (sic) of Glasgow Orpheus Choir fame, who was present, left the auditorium in disgust.

My father's skills lay elsewhere. Incidentally, no mention of my mother (also a teacher) is because in those days, married women were not allowed to teach. The moment she became the wife of Robert Andrew Denoon, my mother had to abandon the profession she had trained so long and hard to join.

My father was a keen gardener, and introduced it as an additional activity and it became popular. Although Abriachan was high in the hills and had fierce winters, the school and its grounds were guarded by a thick, dark pine wood that protected it from the prevailing winds.

In the nineteen thirties, schools in Inverness-shire competed for a trophy called the Soper Cup, for the best school garden. The trophy had been presented by a Colonel Soper. Abriachan won it on two successive occasions. It was around this time that my parents began to realise that their school was regarded in certain areas of community estimation as being some kind of second-class establishment due to the petty slights that could occur. Although the prestigious Soper Cup had been won, there was to be no presentation of the award – either in the school or in the community. Abriachan was very proud of this success, but my father was told by letter by either the director of education or the assistant, that he would have to come to Inverness himself if he wanted to collect the cup. The same crude brush-off for the school occurred the following year when the cup was won again. There would be no official presentation at the school. There was a distinct sense that it was not unconnected with the large number of boarded out children on the roll.

My own memories of these boarded-out pupils is of them being pretty tough – different from us locals. No Queensberry rules for them when it came to a fight, and their accents, savage to our ears, came mainly from the Lowlands and often from Glasgow. These accents intimidated me. Our education was of its times: it was strict and formal and things like the discipline of learning by rote were hard for many to accept. I still have in my memory the image of an older boy, standing beside my father's tall, Victorian desk, being given his last chance to get his Bible homework right. He was having to recite, in the teeth-baring demotic of Glasgow, the lines:

The gates of brass before him burst
The iron fetters yield ...

His ferocious delivery had enough pent-up violence in it to uproot any gates or splinter any fetters trying to restrain him. An early lesson in the street culture of the Dear Green Place for me, perhaps.

A school inspector was once asking them their Catechism. He asked one of the girls how far they had got with it. She replied, "Past *redemption*, over the page, and *into the pains of hell for ever.*" (If you have no idea as to what the Shorter Catechism was, then this will be far over your head. Better leave it there.)

The unpleasantly petty attitude towards Abriachan School also occurred in connection with sport. Here again, the school had been galvanised. There was regular training in running, jumping - all the usual things. The aim was to win the annual inter-school competition between a number of neighbouring primary schools – including one on the outskirts of Inverness. When the Abriachan team appeared, there were gasps. They were all turned out in smart shorts and singlet uniform, with the school sports emblem emblazoned on each. It was a green heart. The idea was my father's – a keen fly fisherman – and was based on the fact that fishing rods in those days were made of greenheart. You could bend it but you couldn't break it. All right, a little bit strained, but it certainly was original.

Anyway, Abriachan won the first sports meeting – yet did not get the trophy. Deep suspicion filled the air. Some pretty selective judging was going on. The school with the boarded-outs was not getting fair treatment from the judges. At the next meeting, which happened to be chaired by the redoubtable Baroness Burton of Dochfour (indeed it was she who had initiated and sponsored this inter-school competition) the matter was brought up by my father. He suggested that it might be better if the Inverness Amateur Athletics officials were to adjudicate in future. The Baroness agreed immediately, and on the next sports day, it was Abriachan who lifted the premier award. Interesting to note that one of the officials that day was the famous Inverness auctioneer, wit and showman, Willie Michie.

There was some bad feeling directed at Abriachan school for this rather public questioning of the organisation of these sports meetings, but that just had to be lived with.

This attitude towards the boarded out pupils was bad enough, but there was a much darker side to this system. Amazing as it might seem, this only came to light towards the end of my father's life when he and my mother were living in retirement on the outskirts of Inverness. There was a ring on their door bell one day. On the step stood a middle-aged man in holiday clothing. His accent was North American.

He asked if my father recognised him. He did not. A little more probing from the stranger to see if he could get a response, and when there was none forthcoming, he told who he was. He had been a pupil at Abriachan and had left just before the war. More details, and then my father began to remember. He could picture a trio of boarded-out pupils – two brothers and their sister. All three had been fostered by a respectable, elderly local couple. After an afternoon of catching up on the many years that had passed, the subject of the Abriachan School days inevitably came up. It began innocently enough when the visitor remarked that the school had been the only place where he and his brother and sister had been really happy in those days. Nice for my father to hear, but the intensity with which the visitor had said it made him inquire further. And it was then that an account of what really lay behind the grey walls of that long-ago respectable house cast a chill over that summer afternoon. Quite simply, these children had been living in a state of constant and unrelieved terror. Summary, barbaric punishments and endless hours of grinding toil, inflicted by people who only saw them as things little better than slaves or beasts of burden. The cruelties were shocking.

After sitting in stunned silence while listening to all of this, my father asked the man why they hadn't complained. There were inspectors who called to see how the boarded out children were being treated in their foster homes. Then there was the school and the teachers there. Surely they could have alerted someone to the monstrous cruelties they were being subjected to.

"Who would have believed us?" was the reply.

And my father and mother were forced to concede – also that they too would have probably dismissed outright any accusations against the household which was supposed to be looking after them. These wretched children had agreed among themselves that any attempt to reveal their desperate plight would only have resulted in making things even worse for them.

Then the visitor told of one occasion when my father and mother had visited the house one afternoon for tea. Confined to the kitchen area, but fascinated by the thought of the headmaster and his wife as guests in the house, those three children had taken it in turns to peer at the guests through the key-hole – a glimpse of the ordinary world to which they were denied entry. Even over the huge span of years, it was eerie to think back to that ordinary front room in Abriachan with the stilted ritual of afternoon tea with those now long-dead people – and it all being watched secretly and intently by that house's helpless and monstrously ill-treated young victims.

The nine Abriachan years came to an end in 1944. It was clear enough, even then, that the school was doomed. The boarded-out system that had sustained it artificially was soon to be discontinued. Curiously, this did not impinge on the old Inverness County Council education authorities who proceeded to build the canteen and dining facilities that were springing around schools all over the land shortly after the end of the war. In spite of the imminent collapse of the Abriachan school roll, these buildings made their appearance. They were scarcely used.

Next for our family was the junior secondary school at Fort Augustus on the western end of Loch Ness. This was a more attractive proposition, even although the village's main dynamic spell in its history still lay a few years ahead with the coming of the hydro-electric schemes in the early fifties. Already, though, the village had a reasonable population and thus potential in educational terms.

Abriachan slipped away, and we quickly adapted to the ways of the people of the plains.

Fort Augustus

Up till this point in the story, my own perception on the events described has been rather limited. I was eight years of age when we left Abriachan to go to Fort Augustus, so that it was only about the latter part of life in our home in the hills that I have firm memories. The rest is made up of tales that I heard from parents down through the years – indeed right up until they died in the early nineties.

I do remember the actual day of the great flitting to Fort Augustus. There were two lorries, I think, to transport all our goods. I travelled in the largest lorry with its tall, upright wooden cab in which I watched the driver heave on the enormous steering wheel as he gingerly pointed the heavily loaded vehicle down the steep brae towards the loch-side far below. I had had an image in my head of the village we were heading for. It was made up out of stray scraps of information from my parents who had obviously been there in advance to survey the schoolhouse and the various amenities of our new home.

I have to say that we were aware – my brother sister and I – that our mother wasn't all that keen on the move. We were to find out why later. But for me at any rate, it was the idea of us now living in a village – a real village – that was so attractive. Abriachan wasn't really a proper one – it lacked a shop and a church and was vague and scattered. Fort Augustus, from the stray scraps of detail that I could glean from my parents' conversations, became in my mind's eye a rather exciting prospect. I could see it as a small town, with a main street and lots of shops. The details that excited me most of all were the large clock tower and the railway station. I could see the clock tower standing over and dominating the centre of the town and ringing out the hours.

Well, most of these details indeed were to be found in Fort Augustus, except that they were not clasped close together in streets and squares. Instead, they were scattered over a fairly wide area. And yes, there was a clock tower, but it rose from the huge bulk of the Benedictine Abbey, which stood aloof from the village. There were two towers. The other one was pointed and had long vanes where were contained the bells that marked the various mysterious points in the Roman Catholic calendar of worship.

The heavy lorry creaked and heaved its lumbering way up the sharp steepness of Bunoich Brae and then up the even steeper entrance into the school playground. At first glance, it looked rather like the building we had left: all Scottish grey stone and tall pointed windows in the gables. My father was there before us. He had gone ahead on his army motor bike. Soon we began to realise why our mother was somewhat muted in her enthusiasm. Even I quickly noted that the rooms were markedly smaller and that there was a shabby wooden annex tacked on to the house at the back door, near the playground. From the start, this was always called the Back Place – a sort of half-way house between the main house and the open air. The floor was of a permanently chilled cement. But soon it was to have a magnificent Rayburn cooker installed that put life (and an efficient hot water system) into what was a very unwelcoming part of our new home.

And now for an unfortunate co-incidence. In the same way as my father had inherited an eccentric regime in Abriachan, so also did he follow an extremely odd head teacher in Fort Augustus. The grimly unwelcoming house was the consequence of the sheer lack of interest the outgoing people had in such things as creature comforts. As far as the actual educational side of matters was concerned, there was the scholastic legacy of a head teacher whose hobby and total obsession was the making of fishing flies. He had an armchair in his classroom, and in its depths every teaching day, he spent his time at this activity. A vast amount of remorseless teaching had to be done to fill the enormous gap in the basic knowledge and skills of the young of Fort Augustus.

We met with kindness there, however, from the moment of our arrival. There was a fire burning in one of the grates, and we were approached by a small, grey-haired lady. She was Mrs Leslie, the wife of the local tycoon grocer, Jesse Leslie, who then lived at Spring Cottage just a couple of doors further up the Brae. She had prepared a welcoming cup of tea for us.

If my parents were not all that keen on their new house – it was smaller overall than the one we had just left in Abriachan – I found the whole set up to be intriguing. Fort Augustus Junior Secondary School with schoolhouse attached, in those days, stood on the small hill called Bunoich that overlooked the village. Behind it rose the bald outcrop of the Battery Rock. "Battery" because the Jacobites had placed a battery of guns there during the Forty Five Rising, and had bombarded the Hanoverian fort that stood where the Abbey now is. There is a mysterious hole drilled in the large round outcrop of rock at the summit – a support for an eighteenth century gun carriage perhaps?

The view from the front of the schoolhouse took in most of the village, and, to the west, the dramatic conical outline of Ben Teigh. Some said that the Ben was the most accurate of weather pointers. If you could see it clearly, then rain was imminent; if you couldn't see it, then it was raining. In fact the weather there was no better nor worse than most other parts of the Highlands, though being in the middle of the Great Glen, you received the full effect of the prevailing wind that funnelled from the west. The schoolhouse was in a lucky situation in that the Battery Rock protected it from the more infrequent, but very unpleasant, chill winds from the east.

But two features of our new home village were quite far beyond my wilder early fantasies: the canal and the railway station. I had heard about the canal, but the concept of boats and ships actually sailing through the middle of the village was totally beyond me. Yet that was what actually happened. But what about the railway station? This was really something else. I had been on trains already at this early age – most notably with my mother to Edinburgh when I can remember seeing the Forth Bridge surrounded by its flotilla of barrage balloons. From the schoolhouse, the vast plumes of steam and smoke could be seen filling the sky as locomotives from Spean Bridge noisily shunted their wagons to be loaded up with timber that was being stripped from the hillsides by the mysterious and taciturn "Newfies", or Newfoundlanders, who worked in the forests then.

Closer inspection of the railway proved a bit of a let-down. Although there was a real station building there with waiting room with posters of seaside resorts far away in England and a ticket office, in fact no passenger trains called here any more. There were only goods trains. The second profound disappointment was that parental decree laid down that I was not to be allowed to go across the village to watch the trains on my own. I can remember having been there, though, probably accompanied by an adult, and for only far too short a time. What I didn't know was that it was really only timber for the war effort that was keeping the station functioning. Shortly after the war ended, so did the railway connection to Fort Augustus. It was very soon after that the actual track was ripped up; making certain that this link was gone for ever. Actually this railway line was only half of what had been a failed venture of a rail link between the two ends of the Great Glen, early in the 20th century. The line had continued for a couple of miles to the east of the village, crossing the River Oich by a spectacular bridge (the pillars of which still stand naked of their metal track-bearing carriageway) and along the loch side on embankments and through cuttings to the pier where the Mathesons used to live.

All my life, I have thought about this railway line. From Spean Bridge to Fort Augustus it must have been stunningly beautiful. A close friend of the family, Eric Birkett, had in his day been a railway enthusiast, and had raved about this journey that he had taken in the nineteen thirties. Actually, the bulk of this line – its bridges and engineering – are still clearly visible from the road alongside Loch Lochy and Loch Oich, high up on the hillsides. What a wonder the Great Glen rail journey would have been if that venture had succeeded in making the link-up with Inverness. Perhaps it might even have avoided the violent attacks of the nineteen sixties when the Beeching savagery saw to the removal of so many picturesque railway lines.

The Parrot from Hell
And
The Village Hall

The war was still on when we arrived in Fort Augustus, and my father was still involved in the Home Guard. This meant that he was frequently away from home on various exercises and manoeuvres. He was now a Lieutenant – but by rights, should have been Captain. However, within the chain of command there existed a rather implacable obstacle to his advancement, so it was as a Lieutenant that he saw the ending of hostilities in 1945, with the first Victory celebrations, VE Day - (Victory in Europe). This was followed later by VJ Day – Victory in Japan. Both of these occasions were celebrated in the village, of course – though the memories of them have become somewhat merged. Each was marked by a huge bonfire on a bare rocky outcrop, above the mouth of the River Oich, just overlooking the railway cutting of the never-completed line to Inverness.

One of these bonfire celebrations was nearly wrecked by bad weather. It was very wet and extremely windy. The fierce gale tore at the bonfire once it had taken hold and sparks and embers were driven horizontally out over the churning surface of the loch. From somewhere or other, someone had got hold of fireworks (how possible in wartime?). Obviously, I had never seen such wonders before, but the impact was spoiled a little by the ferocious wind that snatched each rocket and Roman Candle projectile at its moment of launching and flung it remorselessly out over the loch, into which they would disappear ineffectually. But the huge fires towered redly on both occasions and crowds of villagers pressed round and gazed into their depths while the half-bottles circulated.

I had a strange vision of how the war would end. This vast event was associated absolutely in my mind with parents huddled round the big wooden cabinet of the Marconi wireless set in the living room with its illuminated tuning dial full of mysterious names like Hilversum and even the sinister Berlin. They always seemed to be listening to news. I am told that I observed, one day, "Wouldn't it be great to switch on the wireless one day, and hear the man say, 'There's no news today. The War is over.'" The War had been for all of my sentient life the dominating, gloomy force. It came between me and all the wondrous things that the older people were forever talking about, introducing the topic with the words, "Of course, before the war ..." It was to me a sort of lost paradise – one never to be regained.

Then, to add to the constant torment of being told of the marvels of these wondrous days of long ago, there were still enough reminders lying around of the fact that our elders were indeed telling the truth. There were the characters in comics and story books on tropical islands who were forever eating that pale-yellow, curved fruit with the skin that, when you had peeled it away, lay draped over the hand. You just craved to know what the taste was. But one of the worst of all is one that is still etched deeply in my memory. It was an advertisement for MacVitie's Biscuits. It was in the window of Aitchison's the Bakers shop just across the canal bridge. This advertisement has to be described in detail so that its full effect on wartime children can be appreciated. It was in harsh, primary colours and showed a nineteen thirties family at home. All had pale, polished complexions, like wax fruit. The father had his straight-stemmed pipe clenched tightly in manly jaw as he looked over his newspaper. Mother stood close by with her tight, crinkly-permed cap of hair. A small Shirley Temple in fluffy frock clasped hands in girlish glee. What was it that this smug little nuclear family was looking at so smilingly? They were all looking at the son – a waxen clone of Dad – in shorts and with centre parting in his hair. Beside him was the most gigantic biscuit box in the world. Its lid was off, to reveal a quite stupefying selection of contents. If it had not said it on the side of the box, I really would not have known that they actually were biscuits. No remote resemblance did they bear to what we occasionally could buy in Leslie's the grocers. Dark brown chocolate, twirls of coloured icing toppings and thick-spread custard cream fillings. There were all shapes of smooth, ribbed and tumbled delights – and all packed into that tin that stood full in the centre of the picture. But it was what that boy was doing that was quite beyond the bounds of what the imagination could cope with. He was holding out one of the most tantalising of these biscuit fantasies to a gigantic, hook-beaked parrot on its perch that was deigning to nibble a corner of it.

The loathsome boy wasn't even eating the biscuit himself. He was offering it to a parrot!

But to return to the Victory celebrations. In Fort Augustus – as in all other communities throughout the land – there was yet another celebration being planned. This was the "Welcome Home" for the troops, now demobbed, and the returning prisoners of war. The village hall was packed and everything was laid on for these returning men and women. Dancing and feasting, on the drearily limited things available in those days of extreme austerity. My memory doesn't tell me if I actually witnessed any of this.

But one thing I do remember from this time is that it was the very first occasion that I ever tasted ice cream. How it was made and where it came from, I do not know, because it certainly came into the infuriating "Oh yes, before the war .." category of things never experienced. Anyway, I was in my bed with a cold or flu or something. I knew that there were great things happening in the village hall a few hundred yards up the road, because both of my parents were involved in the organisation. I remember my mother coming into the bedroom with a plain white bowl in her hand and a spoon.

"Would you like to try some of this?"

The expression on my face would have said it all. It looked like something pretty dull and worthy like semolina or sago.

"Come on. Give it a try."

I sat up reluctantly and watched the curiously stiff-looking white stuff being spooned into a dish. It is hard to convey, over the span of the years, the combination of shock and delight that followed the first nervous taste. It broke all the rules of foodstuffs learned up till that moment. These rules were laid down by the austerity of wartime – implacable rules that went with empty shelves and ration books. This was the first true hint that there were better times ahead.

Although we were denied sweet things during the war and the years immediately after, we really craved them. It has to be some instinct in children as opposed to conditioning. In the village in those days, there were two MacDonald's shops, run by members of the same family. They were known as MacDonald's "Top Shop" and ditto "Bottom Shop". The former was the general store, mainly groceries, while the latter was newspapers and bric-a-brac. In happier days, the Bottom Shop was also the village sweetie shop, and it was there that we would go with our coupons for the pathetic amounts that the rationing system allowed us. I can remember one magical day, when there was a government decree that there would be a very brief relaxation of the rationing of sweets. I still remember going into Mrs MacDonald's shop and getting two Mars Bars. Once again, it is well-nigh impossible to convey to the sugar-sated generations that have followed, just what a supreme moment that event was. The credibility gulf is just too wide.

But to return to the village hall. This played quite a large part in our family's life. My father had his moments of glory there in his capacity as producer of plays for the local dramatic society. "Campbell of Kilmhor" and "With Decorum and Economy" are a couple of titles that hover in my memory yet. In fact when I was a bit older I had a couple of walk-on parts myself. In the earlier days in the forties, I would have to say that it was my mother who was the star of stage. When living in Abriachan, she frequently sang at concerts in the small hall there and had a fine singing voice. Unfortunately, her voice became affected by some condition, incurable in those days, and her singing days came to an abrupt end. But she still could play the piano. In Auchterawe, far into the dark forest to the west of the village, lived a crofter called Jock MacLaren. He was a keen fiddler, and had collected a number of local musicians to form MacLaren's Band. There were other fiddlers – and was there an accordionist? – and there was a drummer. There was also a pianist. That was my mother. MacLaren's Band was much in demand, not only in their home village, but also in neighbouring Invermoriston and Invergarry. I would like to think that it was predominantly their skills that had them seem so popular. However, I have more than a suspicion that it was the fact that they didn't charge for their performances that might have played a small part.

We knew the MacLarens well in another capacity. It was from them and their croft that we got a part of our milk supply. This meant a long cycle run up to Auchterawe with an empty milk can clanking from the handlebars on the way there, and then having to be nursed without any milk being spilt all the way back again. Winter journeys down the inky blackness of the tunnels of Forestry trees were occasions of special terror.

It was partly as a result of encouragement from Jock MacLaren that I developed certain skills on the harmonica. These had me – not so much a child prodigy as a child curiosity – performing my repertoire of Scottish dance music on concert stages in Fort Augustus and neighbouring villages. I launched my act with – what else? – Kate Dalrymple. This would be followed by Bonnie Dundee, The Hen's March to the Midden, the Irish Washerwoman – all with as many grace notes crammed in as possible – and the lot rounded up with a final blast of Kate Dalrymple. Jock even lent me a button-key accordion for a spell, but here I had to admit failure. Tunes could be played easily enough, but harmonising with the left hand key-board proved to be totally beyond me.

But I think it was the little navy-blue van that brought the fortnightly film shows to the village that provided one of the most outstanding early memories of that building. (I have further ones connected with later years when I was old enough to attend the dances there myself.) It was driven by a raffish-looking character who had been a member of air-crew in the RAF during the recent war. The organisation was called the "Highlands and Islands Film Guild". Now, there was no electricity at our side of the canal at this time, before the coming of Hydro electricity, so there was a small petrol engine in the back of the van which turned the generator which in turn supplied the power for the projector. The result of this was that all the films we watched were accompanied by the thudding of this highly unreliable pest of a machine just outside the front door of the hall. There would be a wave of frustration and rage in the audience when, in the middle of some scene of high drama, or an episode of "The Three Stooges" (how unfunny these seem today!), the engine note would falter then splutter and die, making the heroine's voice descend into a low growl while image and sound both disappeared. The Film Guild man would rush outside and wrestle with the engine while someone held his torch. He usually managed to get the thing going again, and I have only one recollection of us actually having to get our money back. It should have been an ideal job for a man who had risked his life over enemy skies, but it was blighted by a two-stroke engine that had a deep malevolence towards humanity built into it.

The Local Grocery Tycoon

I have already mentioned that the very first person to welcome us to Fort Augustus was Mrs Leslie. She was the wife of the local grocer, Jesse Leslie, whose shop stood dead in the middle of the village, right at the point where the main road crosses the canal at the swing bridge. That same building still stands there, basically the same as it was in those days, though with the various extensions that have been added to accommodate our vastly changed shopping habits. Look up at the gable next time you pass the shop. High up, you can still see a large, faint circle – now blank. That circle used to contain the advertising slogan of Leslie's chain of grocery stores that at one time extended from Fort William in the west to Inverness in the east, with a branch in every main village between throughout the length of the Great Glen. At the height of his empire's powers, I believe there was also a branch in Tain – as well as a large wholesaler's business in Inverness and a fine delicatessen. The slogan that was aimed at the passer-by was "Leslie's Stop the Spot to Shop". Both of my parents would go on about this cheerfully ungrammatical exhortation as only teachers of English could. To them it ought to have been: "Leslie's (comma) stop (full stop) (Capital Letter) This is the Spot at which you may shop." Remember that every sentence has to have a verb. Oh yes – and there ought to be a colon instead of a full stop after "stop". The clinically correct version rather lacks the punch of the original it has to be said.

What Jesse Leslie might have lacked in grammatical skills he certainly made up in business acumen. Although the MacDonald family dominated the west side of the canal with the other grocery shop and the newspaper and confectionary shop, with respect to them, it was the Jesse Leslie machine that had the J R Ewing touch of single-mindedness and drive in the world of business and expansion.

When we arrived in the village this was still somewhat in the future – but Leslie's energy was already very much in evidence. The original shop he had set up in the village stood beside the old timber bridge that spanned the River Oich, several hundred yards downstream from the stone bridge that supplanted it when the new road was built in the nineteen thirties. Leslie's new shop was sited in the best position in the village. Our new home in the lee of the Battery Rock commanded a stupendous view of the whole of the village and a marvellous vista along the Great Glen to the west. The building in view, right to the centre of all of this was Leslie's shop. My mother was always a bit of an ad hoc sort of provider for the household in terms of groceries and our lives, now that we lived in a village that actually had shops (unlike Abriachan), and our lives were dominated by constant trips down to Leslie's to top up on vital items. Now, all this last-minute shopping that characterised our household was made easier because Leslie himself spent by far the greater part of his life in his shop. All that was required was a glance across the village to see if there was a light shining from the skylight in the roof over the store area at the back of the shop. If there was, and it nearly always was the case, a bike would sweep down Bunoich Brae, carrying either me or my brother to rattle on the black, paint-blistered door to be admitted. Never in my recollection were you ever turned away. Business, no matter what the hour, was business.

Jesse Leslie himself was, I think, one of the most dapper men I have ever seen. In the shop he was, of course, always in his white overalls, but see him on his way to church: dark-suited, with light homburg hat at a jaunty tilt, and with his slightly high-coloured complexion, he was the absolute epitome of the sharp business gent of those days. In its way, the village was rather proud of him, especially when he had added the shops at Invermoriston, Invergarry,

Spean Bridge and Fort William to his list. Drumnadrochit was already his and later came two businesses in Inverness: Mitchell and Craig (purveyor of fine foods to the gentry on Academy Street) and a large warehouse wholesale business in the warren of long-vanished little streets behind the railway station near Falcon Square. I certainly know that it made me feel a little bit superior that it was someone from our village whose name was prominent in all of those communities along the whole length of the Great Glen. Never would we pass through Fort William for example without looking out for the familiar name and its famous slogan.

Jesse Leslie didn't get where he did by being careless with money. In my early days of acquisitiveness I also craved cash in my pocket, and one day plucked up the courage to ask him if I could have a job as a message boy. I had seen an enormous message bike propped up at the back of the shop, and was overwhelmed by a desire to be like some of the characters in the "Dandy" or the "Beano" and to whistle cheerfully up to people's back doors with groceries piled up in the basket out front. I seem to remember that there was a faint whiff of disapproval from the parents, but this didn't last too long when earnings began to help with the pocket money. The experience was to teach me a basic lesson about life and human nature. I learned that if you have a commodity that is yearned after by an element of the public, then you can fix your price in direct proportion to that yearning. Complaints? There won't be any. I had a craving to ride that huge black bike with the welded-on struts that formed the basket that looked for all the world like the bonnet of a car to be steered. Leslie knew this. So it was that after my first Saturday afternoon and evening of delivering boxes of groceries all over the village, I was looking forward to holding out my hand for a satisfying clink of coins for my pay. I was less than amused when I was pointed towards a baker's tray, which had a scattering of left-over cakes and buns on it. I was told that I could take what I wanted. Luckily this miserable payment method didn't last too long and some cash began to appear. Mind you, it was a pretty miserable scatter of coins that you would get from him. Many, many times over the years, from the earliest days when I heaved my way along on that monstrous bike to the more mature times after I had passed my driving test, and could drive one or other of the more tattered of Leslie's fleet of vans – on many of these occasions I would stand, late on a Saturday night, with miles and miles of narrow country roads negotiated, and stare in disbelief at the miserable huddle of coins in the cup of my palm. But I always came back, and that mysterious compact between the exploiter and the exploited continued. Yes, I knew I was being exploited, but only because the lust for getting behind the steering wheel of a vehicle overcame all common sense. Great commercial empires flourish on the tacit complicity between the user and the used. Leslie's grocery empire was no different.

I do not bear him the tiniest grudge. Some of my happiest memories of those days working for the grocery tycoon of the Great Glen include staring fixedly down the uncertain beam of headlights into inky darkness through the windscreen of a lurching, echoing van while steering it desperately along a twisting thread of road going to, perhaps, Glen Quoich where the engineers in charge of the vast dam that was being built there in the fifties were waiting for me to deliver their supplies. In this camp, my favourite cousin Joan stayed. She was a secretary who had given up a job in the heart of government in London where she regularly rubbed shoulders with the mighty of those days in order to come to this very wildest part of the Highlands. I would have tea and chat with her before the hazardous drive back to Fort Augustus.

And without the absurdly ill-paid job with Leslie's, I would not have that amazing image still fixed in my memory of when I stopped the van at a passing place on the private road to Glendoe Lodge. It was a calm winter moonlit night, and I found myself staring in disbelief at the tidal wave of thick mist that had rolled over and settled in the Great Glen, covering its lower slopes and leaving the two towers of the Abbey standing out as if from below a vast pale flood.

Leslie's was only a Saturday job for me. It was the Forestry Commission that was main employer of youth in those days.

I shall be dealing with this topic at greater length later on, but a brief summary of its main features won't do any harm.

It involved a wide range of actual jobs: weeding in the plant nurseries, planting trees, cutting bracken on the hillsides to allow the young trees to develop, pruning the lower branches from standing timber, felling timber, gathering statistics for calculating the cubic volume of timber on a hillside – these were the main ones. Other smaller tasks could emerge on the whim of the forester or ganger. The Forestry could train you to adapt to the numbing tedium of tasks that were uncomfortable, repetitive and during which all time seemed to stand fixed and still. Jobs when the yearning for the tea break seemed to push its arrival further and further into the far distance.

But it is the positive that is to be stressed. At a relatively early age, we were brought into contact with the work ethic and drawn into a vast institution with all its inherited values and rules. And it has left me with many memories of places in the open hills with their spectacular views far away from the narrow constricting roads far below. I worked in the Forestry Commission not only in the summer and Easter holidays, but also in the winter as well. The view from a promontory overlooking Loch Ness between Invermoriston and Fort Augustus, near Christmas time, when I came on a large holly tree in a clearing that was almost sagging with the weight of its scarlet berries, for example. Snow lay on the ground and the sky was dazzling blue. It was completely silent. I have not the faintest idea as to the reason for me being there on that day or why I should have been alone, but it is something fixed impermeably in my memory that can bring back the warmth of links with early home at winter holiday time. It clearly was in student days that this encounter took place.

The main thing about the Forestry Commission in those days was that there was always work available for us. I have no recollection of ever having been turned away from the green wooden office up the Auchterawe road when looking for holiday employment. It always seemed to be granted. It was mainly boys who were taken on, but some local girls were included in our squad. But only for work in the extensive nurseries for the infant trees and weeding the seed beds. I am certain they didn't venture up into the hills for the other tasks.

Another job, an occasional one this time in winter, was the postie's one at Christmas. As a result of that brief experience – I only did it twice I think – even up till this late stage in my life, I NEVER ask my postie, should I meet him some distance from my house, "anything for me today?" And the reason for this reticence? Well, when I had sorted out the letters for my round in Mrs Cameron's cramped little Post Office by the Canal side in Fort Augustus, and bundled them all into my big canvas bag in the strict order in which I would deliver them, I used to seethe with sulphurous fury when someone would approach me with cheerful breeziness and ask if there was anything in the post today? It meant that I had to burrow deep into the bag, disturbing all my meticulous sorting out and knocking my preparations askew. Once I suggested to just such an inquirer that I'd prefer if she'd wait till I had put it through her letter box and was delivered of a sharp rebuke for my lack of courtesy. So that is why the postie on my round today will never get that request from me. I have felt his pain.

Shinty - and the Lay Preacher

When I was a pupil in Fort Augustus, one of the real difficulties was the fact that I was taught at some point or other by both of my parents. Not something I would recommend. The reasons are pretty obvious. You do not always step through a green door into a totally separate world as Graham Greene did in his father's school. All too often you found school glaring back at you across the table after a particularly traumatic day at history or mental arithmetic with one or other of the parents.

"Leave the table, and don't come back till you can say the twelve times table."

It didn't happen all that often, but it was an ever-present danger.

There was another danger – the chance that certain of the school tearaways would take it out on you if they had been belted for something or other. There was the day when Scousie had been at the receiving end of a severe thrashing from my father, and set about dishing out the same to me at the school gate at four o'clock. He was older than I and there wasn't too much that I could do against his assault. Afterwards, of course, there was no clyping, and the age-old excuses were trotted out when I was back in the house, to explain away my altered features. But, on the whole, this didn't become a significant feature in any of our lives – that's my brother and sister too.

Shinty in those days played a large part in life, both in and out of school. The game already had its roots firmly planted in the village long before we arrived there but as in other communities, had faded during the war years. My father had played shinty in his own school days and then in Edinburgh University in the nineteen twenties. His sternly dignified presence looked down on us from the photographs of triumphant teams, through their veils of sepia. Students in his day seemed to have a greater gravitas and maturity about them – certainly as seen through the lens of the camera. I might digress for a moment here: a small mystery that has popped its head up. He had been a pupil in Balnain Primary School, several miles up Glenurquhart and then later in the secondary school at Drumnadrochit. I had always assumed that he would have been through his shinty nursery at Balnain, to have it honed later in the secondary school. Not a bit of it. None of the boys played shinty at Balnain – indeed had scarcely even heard of it in the spell between 1912 and 1918. It wasn't until they came under the ferocious tutelage of Fraser (nicknamed the "Broch") in Drumnadrochit, that shinty was introduced to them. Now, Glenurquhart was right in at the beginning of the formalising of the rules of the game in the late nineteenth century and some of our family's ancestors can be identified in teams that took part in early, titanic clashes. So, what happened to shinty for a brief spell in that part of Glenurquhart that could have seen the game virtually disappear from the consciousness of the young? That conundrum, I leave to others to unravel.

But shinty soon came back into its own in Fort Augustus again and my father must take a bow for the part he played in this. Apart from organising it in the school, and becoming a member of the Schools Camanachd Association, he also became involved in the senior village team during its existence as Fort Augustus and later when it linked up with Invergarry under the name Inveroich. He decided that it might be a good idea to have a sort of school league competition, but with just two teams. One was called Bunoich after the hill on which the school stood and it was made up of players from the east side of the canal. The other team was called Market Hill and was drawn from the west side. How you could regret that so and so's parents didn't live on our side instead. The two teams were kitted out properly from funds that came probably from a sale, and were as follows: Bunoich, Hibs-style green and white with white shorts and Market Hill, red tops with navy blue shorts.

On paper, at any rate, Bunoich seemed to have the advantage. After all, we had the skills of the immensely fit and lithe Camerons from Portclair: Roddy, Donnie and Jimmy. Also the MacDonalds from Auchterawe – especially the powerful compactness of Alan MacDonald. Other names from either side still hover in the memory: the Aitchisons, Morrisons, Wisharts – and the mightily skilled captain of Market Hill, Jimmy Henderson from Glendoe. Where, oh where, are they all now?

It's amazing whenever an artificial division is made in a community how quickly people become fired with primitive passions. The intensity of the atmosphere at these matches on the field at the old Piggery Park was quite astonishing. Large crowds lined the pitch and the game was contested against the background of shrill screams from mothers of players and the hoarse bellowings of fathers as well as the many others who turned up. Our goalkeeper for Bunoich was Roy Mackenzie. I will carry with me for ever the image of his frantic mother who positioned herself right beside the goal, drenching him in torrents of advice and exhortation. Once he sped out beyond the circle to try to intercept a Market Hill attack, leaving his goal unguarded. There was a spell of scuffling and confusion with the goalkeeper still far away from his position. Roy's mother just could not contain herself, and she leapt into the goal to deputise for her son, yelling at him to Get back! Get back! I have no idea how the referee handled that situation, but it does indicate the level of community involvement in this competition. The cup that we were playing for was the Aitchison Cup – presented by the local bakery family. I have no idea who won it more often, but I do have a feeling that it was Bunoich. Some veteran from these days might remember it as otherwise.

One of my own shinty heroes of those days was also a good friend of the family. His name was Willie Jack. His elderly widowed mother lived just down the road from us, across the main road and just under and beyond the old railway bridge. I used to visit her every Sunday to swop one of our Sunday newspapers for her "Sunday Post" which had Oor Wullie and the Broons. Just inside her tiny front porch, above the coat-stand, hung a beautiful ebony-black, silver-mounted presentation caman, with which her son had been presented as a North Select winning captain in 1939. Now and again, she would take it down to let me handle it in dumb reverence. Willie had been wounded in the war and his best shinty-playing days were behind him when I saw him play, but he still possessed amazing skills and that economy of movement that is the hall-mark of all true artists in their chosen game.

No need to say that the Church also played its important part in life then – as did Sunday school. We were regular attenders of both and accepted them with a sort of dull resignation. Weekend visits to grandparents brought no relief. Equally remorseless attendance there as well. An extraordinary episode then punctuated this pattern of life in our family. For reasons too baroque and complex to enlarge upon here, my father gave up attending the Church of Scotland with the rest of us, and re-admitted himself to the Free Church.

Actually, I think I will tell the background after all. When I was a student in Aberdeen University, I was astounded when I opened a newspaper one day to find a headline along the lines of "North Headmaster Throws Pupils Out Into Winter Snow". A scrutiny of the accompanying text revealed that the Head Teacher of Fort Augustus JS School had been doing just that: refusing to let the children stay inside the building when there were howling blizzards outside. As presented by the newspaper, my father was a singularly unpleasant person indeed and was held up as so by the editorial. I phoned home immediately and found that sulphurous wrath was emanating from the schoolhouse. And the object of this wrath was Rev Hugh Gillies, the Church of Scotland minister. What had happened was that Rev Gillies was a member of the Education Committee for the county, and in that capacity had been trying to indicate that it was high time there was money allocated to Fort Augustus School for the provision of a proper shelter for the pupils. To illustrate how bad things were, he had suggested (with a certain exaggeration) that pupils had to endure severe discomfort during the winter months. A reporter had embellished this tale for the sake of a wildly inaccurate headline and story. The damage was done, and it was too late for the hapless Rev

Gillies to protest his innocence. It was a misunderstanding, of course, but a rather damaging one. It was to be some time before the Manse/Schoolhouse friendship was re-established.

My father had been brought up within the embrace of the Free Church in Glenurquhart. He had become disillusioned with it during his spell as head teacher in Elgol in Skye. Now, the Fort Augustus Free Church and Manse were quite close to the schoolhouse and the minister there was the Reverend MacLeod. His poor health meant that sometimes he was not able to take the services and on these occasions a lay preacher would deputise. One of these lay preachers came from Invergarry. Memory can be a deceptive and unreliable faculty, but in this man I can still see each and every trait and feature of the most archetypal Calvinist lay preacher that Scotland's grim religious crucible has ever brought forth. I can see a long, dark coat, a wide-brimmed hat and long, grey and utterly humourless features. All of this was the repository of the most sonorous, Old-Testament-intoning voice ever to lay its hellfire-relishing threats over a cowed and cringing congregation. I was once asked to drive him to Invermoriston to take a service in the school there – and I had no means of escape. The final touch was that he was totally and utterly tone-deaf, and his full-throated bellowing of the Metric Psalms was something that Torquemada himself would have happily added to his canon of tortures for his enemies.

My father soon discovered for himself the special purgatory of a two-hour stint with the Lay Preacher in the pulpit, and began to regret his switch from the benign presiding of the Reverend Hugh Gillies in the Church of Scotland. This developed into a weekly Russian Roulette as to whether the Free Church service would be taken by the Reverend MacLeod or his deadly Invergarry substitute. Then, one day, the obvious solution. The bus stop was clearly visible from the schoolhouse, so it was just a matter of watching, through binoculars, and studying the passengers alighting, watching for the give-away dark exclamation mark of the presence of the Lay Preacher. If he appeared, then no church that Sunday for my father. Then disaster struck from a blue sky. The binoculars had been trained on the bus and the emerging passengers close to Grant's Garage. No sign of the enemy, so off up the brae went my father towards the church. When he still hadn't returned after the passing of an hour and a half, we

knew that something had gone terribly wrong. Yes, my father's Nemesis had got a lift that Sunday, and had been driven directly to the church. He even greeted my aghast father on his way in with his lugubrious, "Good morning, Mester (sic) Denoon."
There was no possible escape.
The only immediate change in tactics was that my father found another vantage point from which his sweep of the binoculars could cover both the bus stop and the door of the Free Church, before daring to set forth.

It was a huge relief to all of us when the temporary rift with the Church of Scotland was healed, though the loss of the potential humour was regretted. The stumbling walk, the nervous twitch and the ashen features of a man who had sat through two hours of the Lay Preacher in full flow was a sight never to be forgotten, but it didn't get all that much sympathy from the rest of us in the family.

The Fort Scout Troop

On the 28th June, 1947, when I was ten years of age the Fort Scout Troop was inaugurated.
It had Three Laws:
Be Partners
Be Polite
Be Punctual
..and its salute and sort of Masonic recognition sign was a truly odd-looking depression of the two middle fingers by the thumb to allow the two remaining fingers, the index and the pinkie, to stick up like small horns.
There were two patrols: the Blue Patrol and the Red Patrol. Each had its Morse Code call signal: dash-dot for Red and dash-dot-dash-dot for Blue.

You will by now have gathered that I am not describing a branch of Lord Baden Powell's Boy Scout movement here. No Canadian Mountie hats or neckerchiefs or woggles for us in the Fort Scout Troop. No, we were the brief and flickering creation of a next-door neighbour on Bunoich Brae – Captain Searight, who was a lodger with Mrs Cottington. I think he was one of the many eccentric teachers who were drawn to the Benedictine private boarding school in the Abbey in those days – single military or naval men, finding a haven there from former lives of action in defence of empire. Whatever his background, lost now to any feasible research, *(though a quick search by the miracle of Google has revealed a Captain Arthur Kenneth Searight of the Royal West Kent Regiment who was decorated in the First World War. I wonder?)* Captain Searight was a man driven by an urge to organise, to codify and to list things in life. I know this, because in my parents' house, I once stumbled across a faded, stiff-covered sort of school science note-book, with all of the pages in the form of graph paper. On the cover was printed INTELLIGENCE NOTES, SCOUTS.
Inside, the first part of this notebook was given over to wartime information relating to the organisation of the local Home Guard. If the Captain was not a prominent member of that force, then, judging by the contents of that book, he certainly ought to have been. In fact, he was the I.O. or Intelligence officer. If the Nazis had ever invaded

and gained possession of this book, they would have found themselves in possession of details of everyone of note in the community, their status in the defence structure, whether they owned cars, what make they were, their telephone numbers and a host of other small details. There are pages of large-scale maps of the village and the surrounding glens and straths – all of this done in the most intricate and detailed fashion, in blue, red and black ink. The names and all details are written in the tiniest and most elegant of handwriting. It might not seem of too great importance to the social history of the Highlands, but I have to hand at the moment the names of the messengers who would have to run with communications between the various groups of the Home Guard who were battling against the Nazi invaders. I find it quite intriguing because I can remember who many of them were. These lists were compiled before our family moved to Fort Augustus, but some were pupils in the school where I soon got to know them. There was David Leslie, born in December 1929, aged fourteen and eight months. His identity number was SZOL 1/142 and he lived in Spring Cottage. Hugh Wishart, born on 24th October 1931, aged thirteen – identity number SZBD 39/2. He lived in Battery Rock Cottage – and so on and so on.

The list of Available Cars speaks loudly of the social structure of a Highland village in those now-distant days. Really no surprises, it has to be said. Local successful business men like MacDonald the grocer with his 1938 Ford, (Registration Number ST 9914) and D. MacDougall the butcher with his 1939 Austin (Registration Number AST 235) both owning recent but basic vehicles – new but not in any way ostentatious. Further down the redoubtable Captain Searight's list we find Mr Bruen of Ardachy Lodge with a ten horse power Lanchester – a truly solemn and dignified vehicle. Then Mrs Beckett of Cullachy appears with her sixteen horse power Humber, and can you imagine Mr MacGregor living in a house called "Ravensdale" owning anything less eye-catching than a Jowett? Right at the end of this long list comes Miss Fegan of Cullachy with a Vauxhall 10 that is classified as "unlicensed". All the long-ago names of makes of cars: Rileys, Hillmans, Standards and Armstrong-Siddeleys are there, and Fort Augustus seems to have been a reasonably mobile community in those days.

But to return to the main subject of interest from this old, faded notebook of the Captain's – the Fort Scout Troop. The basic statistics tell it all as far as the ephemeral nature of this movement was concerned. But, first of all, what we would refer to as "the image" of the Troop, today? What an Enid Blyton world of French windows, private boarding schools and muffins for tea is summed up by the "Three Laws"! A collection of boys from a Highland village in those days – or at any other time – could hardly be expected to be enthused by that limp list of the Captain's. "Be Punctual"; "Be Polite", for God's sake, when our urgings then leaned towards guns and the echoes of the violence of the recently-ended war. Then there was that salute! Just try it out as per my earlier description and then hold the right hand to the side of the head in saluting mode. Try to look dignified. Not much chance, is there?

When I first looked at the progress reports of the two Patrols, I naturally homed in on my own name. It was actually quite unnerving – my long-ago assessment by someone I had completely forgotten, of my conduct, deportment and skills in activities now completely erased from my memory. And there I was: number five in the Red Patrol, in between Roy Mackenzie and Pat Aitken. All appear to have had some sort of code name. Mine was BRAN. The Captain's eye was on us all of the time. We were being assessed in Observing, Tracking, Reports, PL's Scheme (whatever that was), Movement Reports and Observation Reports – all of these on the five successive weeks of this strange hybrid troop's existence, before it folded up on the 2nd of August, with its total funds standing at two shillings and four pence. The Captain certainly wasn't in it for the money. A series of cryptic symbols against our names told if we were punctual, late "for parade", absent with (or without) a reason, keen, good, fair, ordinary, slack, inattentive – or just plain bad. Points were allocated accordingly. To my relief, I saw that I had managed to amass fourteen points by the week of dissolution – even although on three of those weeks I was absent "with a reason". I then saw that my Troop Leader, Roddy Paterson, had 26. Yet he had almost perfect attendance. And he was fifteen years of age to my ten. How on earth was this possible? Clearly there was no evidence in my points total of any signs of genius or outstanding leadership qualities. Then a look at the Captain's quaint marking system explained all. For being absent "with a reason" you were allocated two points; "without a reason" earned none. So on the three successive weeks I was NOT there, I was awarded six magnificent points. "Late on parade" earned one point, while for a simple "present on parade", three points were awarded. If only such a marking system had accompanied me throughout life, what successes and riches would have accumulated to me.

The whole six-week episode does look a bit sad now – all those crisply annotated pages, evidence of a meticulously obsessive man with an urge to organise local youth. The steady and inexorable falling-off of attendance showed that we had seen through the empty promise of it all. Of the seventeen of us who had enrolled on 28th June 1947, only six managed to make it "on parade" on the 2nd August. I don't know whether I should be proud or not to find I was one of them.

Primary Care

Primary education was, of course, strict and formal in the late forties and early fifties. I know, because the teacher I had for most of it was my own mother. She had been forbidden by the system, in the thirties after she got married, to continue teaching. No married women were permitted in the profession. The realities of recruiting after the war and the dire shortages there were meant that this bit of blatant chauvinism had to be put aside. She joined the staff of the Primary Department in Fort Augustus Junior Secondary School. There was one other teacher in Primary who took the infant sections, a tall kindly young woman called Miss Morrison. I have no memories of an unpleasant nature from her care and tutelage, but when I went to the middle classroom where my mother was in charge, it was a bit different. High standards were expected from me, and high standards were forced out. The most fearsome of the daily events was the spelling test (the list for homework had to be perfect in recollection) and the mental arithmetic quick-fire question sessions. Spelling didn't bother me too much, but the other was pure purgatory. Having said that, I do remember a sort of strange aesthetic satisfaction from arithmetic – in particular the various sums (addition, subtraction etc) in which money was calculated. Pounds, Shillings and Pence, with their formal layout on the page or the blackboard; the shapes of the symbols, the two dots that were placed between the columns of figures, and that calm satisfaction when the neat lines were drawn under the answer. Only those sums that included calculations of farthings and other divisions of the basic penny were not so pleasant. The rest, to my best recollection, was reasonable. I have especial warm memories of history lessons from a textbook that was filled with highly patriotic illustrations. They showed us Scotland in the early days, when our land was throwing off the yoke of domination by our neighbours to the south. The struggles of William Wallace and the triumph of Robert Bruce enthralled us, and it was only when the book took us up to the events of 1707, when the Scots Parliament met for the last time and voted itself out of existence, that there was a distinct sense that something was not right. The illustration I can still remember – a black line drawing of the last session of the Parliament in Edinburgh, and of the great ones of the day moving in procession through the streets of the capital. It should not have happened that way, was the feeling that I, at any rate, felt so strongly. The book didn't tell us more than the facts, but you felt that history had let you down – badly.

Now, what I did not know in those days – and what I only learned many years later – was that my mother, as a student in Edinburgh in the twenties, had been secretary of the University Scottish Nationalists at a time when the party of that name was asserting itself in the land. She met and conversed with the great names of the day, including Compton Mackenzie, and I am sure she mentioned the great Cunninghame-Graham ("Don Roberto", as he became nicknamed because of his astonishingly patrician appearance and travels and adventures in Argentina). In fact, it was a university friend of my mother's who eventually married Compton Mackenzie. So, maybe there was more than a co-incidence in the choice of that particular history book with its powerful illustrations. Certainly it had quite a profound influence on me. And here it is too that the weird schizophrenia of Scotland emerged. At the very moment we were with Bruce and his brave companions in the taking of the various castles of Scotland from the English in the years leading up to the Battle of Bannockburn, we were sitting at our desks in a classroom that had a large map of the world dominating it and visible every time you raised your head. The huge area of it that was coloured red to indicate the British Empire had our little breasts swell with pride. I can remember looking with such regret at the United States with their dull green colouring immediately below the huge swathe of red for Canada – raging inwardly at the crass folly of the Hanoverian monarchy that had been stupid enough to lose them to the rebels. How marvellous if the whole of North America had been red. How it was possible to reconcile these emotions I do not know. I do remember that there was a flag pole in front of the school, but I honestly can say that I have no recollection of any parades on Empire Day, or stuff like that.

When my mother began teaching again, with great enthusiasm, she found that she required some additional help in the house. So it was that one of the girls from the large Cameron family from Port Clair, Margaret, who had just left school, became effectively our maid in the schoolhouse. She actually lived in, and had her own tiny room upstairs, just across the landing from my parents' bedroom. Because she was so young, she became as much a companion to the three of us, and on the occasions that my parents went out visiting friends in the village, we would have many illicit evenings of jollification. The parents never suspected a thing. These visits often had them going down to the Abbey, where they had come to know various members of the staff of the private school there. One of them was an extraordinary man called Wilfred Worden. He was a pianist who had entertained huge audiences as a child prodigy in London – from which city he came. He was also a composer and an inventor. One of his inventions was a record turntable that worked on a completely different principle to the standard kind with its fixed pivot and arm that just moved across the record in what was really an arc. His theory was that the needle ought to pass over the record in a precise straight line, and to achieve this, he had designed and built an arm that was articulated, in order to do just this. It meant that the needle was always exactly perpendicular in the groove of the record. He had quite enormous loudspeakers in his room embedded, if I remember, in sections of earthenware piping to create even greater resonance. Now, I have never since come across this device, but I later heard a rumour to the effect that this patented idea of Wilfred Worden's was such a threat to the huge manufacturers of record decks in those days that they managed to suppress the invention. That's what I was told anyway, and you have to admit that it makes a great story. I did see the device and his gigantic loudspeakers in his room at the Abbey. As a teacher though, he just didn't have any of the necessary qualities. He could be impatient and waspish – as my brother and sister found out to their sustained and intense misery. They were made by our parents to take weekly piano lessons, which they loathed with a profundity that was absolute. Their teacher was short-tempered and utterly unable to provide anything approaching an atmosphere suitable for learning. The irony of all this is that at that time, I was the member of the family who had shown some musical talent. I refer you back to my concert performances on the harmonica.

Looking back, it is quite extraordinary the amount of freedom we had in those days – freedom, that is, to wander far from home and to explore the woods the moors and the rivers that were in abundance around us. The MacDonald family from Auchterawe began, I seem to remember, the custom of coming to school in the summer time, barefooted. Just to imagine the length of the hard and dusty road that lay between their home and the school reminds of the stamina and resolve that this involved. Those of us living nearer had to adopt this style also, and I can remember being amazed at how the feet became accustomed to not having them protected by leather soles. We played our basic and brutish games in our bare feet as well. Although my father was encouraging shinty in the school, there was none played in the playground – for the obvious reason that there were many windows around that would be in danger. Also it was far too small. We had one strange quite fierce game, which had the quite idiotic name of "Kinghornie" and a variation called "Kinghornie with the Ball". One of us became "it" and had to touch any one of the milling mass surging around, who were all trying to avoid you. As each one was touched, he (and I am pretty sure that these games were segregated, although there were no separate playgrounds at Fort Augustus) had the power immediately to touch others – all of whom were joined by hand, till there might be one or two final ones who were hunted down by the huge swinging, joined-up line of the rest of us. It was wonderful and it was chaotic looking but it had its own logic and rules and was very satisfying. The variation "with the ball"

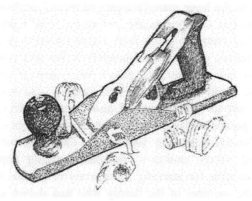

had the one who was "it" throwing a ball, instead of trying to touch, and those thus touched, joined the increasing numbers of the "its" till one or two remained who had to be struck by the ball thrown by one of the rest of us.

Soon after the war, schools all over the country had additional classrooms built alongside them - the famous HORSA Huts. Fort Augustus had its compliment. There were two large ones, and a canteen where the cooks prepared the meals. The dining room doubled as the woodwork room, where the amazing Ewan MacQueen taught the boys woodwork. He was an itinerary teacher of the subject, and came to Fort Augustus once a week. He was stocky and had the most extraordinary, fierce-looking red face that ought to have been terrifying to young people, but to offset that, he had a pawky humour behind the sternness that made the subject reasonably enjoyable. Certainly it was marvellous to be allowed to saw through wood and to plane it smooth with expensive looking tools. His voice was slow and came from the back of the throat, and he had a slight stammer as well. His threats to keep us in line included the admonition that the next one to do such and such a misdemeanour would "be given the t-t-t-t timber.." which meant being swatted in the nether regions with a piece of wood. This was a very rare event, it has to be said. He was well-known throughout much of the Highlands as a lay preacher and fervent member of the strictest denomination of the Presbyterian Church. The Letters Pages of local newspapers for many years would carry his stern strictures on the follies of modern life – each of those letters beginning with a fulsome string of quotations (all identified by chapter and verse) and then going on to condemn the latest folly of our weak and fallible human species.

Before the dining room was built, the meals prepared in the canteen were served and eaten in the actual classrooms. It was a quite marvellous treat. Classrooms were places where knowledge was imparted, and where the world of food and bodily appetites was barred. Yet, when this new part of our school day first made its appearance, we were amazed to see a pile of small, green and white checked plastic covers appearing. They were exactly the size of our desk tops, which had little wooden pegs under the lids which, when raised, would keep the desk top horizontal and level. The small covers then became miniature table-cloths. The cooks would then come in with the large, flat grey containers with soup, stews or mince, potatoes and whatever pudding might be on offer that day. It was the idea of sitting in a classroom and eating a full, midday meal that really excited us all then. Yes indeed, the school meals service was a wonderful thing to those who were there at its inception.

One downside of the school canteen for my father came about as follows. One of the cooks who ran the kitchen always seemed to be trying to be exceptionally nice to him. Nothing too awkward about that, but it became a little problematic when it came to the weekly treat of the Jam Tart. This was the favourite pudding of, I think, all of us. Certainly it was as far as I was concerned. The only slight snag is that on alternate weeks, instead of the fiercely artificial red of the jam that was spread over it, it would be the pale yellow of a substance that not only have I always disliked, but has, frankly, puzzled me. Why question "why?" is uppermost. It was lemon curd. However, I digress. This head cook, in order to ingratiate herself with the headmaster, would always see that he was specially favoured when the tart was being cut up and dispensed. She had a knack of making the pastry with an enormous, knuckle of extra dough around the edges, and especially at the corners. For some reason, it was from the corner that my father's enormous portion was taken, and after its copious drenching in the standard issue, industrial strength custard of the day, it was lovingly placed before him. He was never too keen on pastry, and this enormous soggy helping of it was a special purgatory to him. He was visible to the whole of the gathering, and could not be seen to leave any scrap on his plate, so it was duly disposed of. I cannot remember how this problem was finally resolved.

Next in this random visiting of stray memories of my Primary School days, I have to mention another oddity. This pre-dates the coming of the school meals service. It was an early attempt by the powers that be to give school pupils additional vitamins – in the form of a chocolate powder that was made into a hot drink. The powder came in huge, shiny tins, and one part of the daily ritual was the lifting into the classroom by the teacher of a truly gigantic iron kettle filled with cold water. This was placed in the middle of the fire that burned in the grate at the front of the room. We would watch and listen, since it was always timed to be boiling just when it was interval time at around eleven o'clock. When the steam was rushing from the spout and the lid was bumping up and down, then it was interval. We all had our own mugs, and queued up to have heaped spoonfuls of this light-brown powder put in, and then the mug topped up with the boiling water. I remember that there was no sugar (or milk) added, but that the drink was sufficiently sweet not to require any. Neither was the milk missed. In fact, it was a very pleasant drink to have on a chilly winter morning, in classrooms that had only the fire in the grate as a source of heat.

We were always told how important it was to be at our very best when the school inspectors visited. Needless to say, we were made to believe it that it was we who were being inspected. No idea did we have that it was those who were running the school whose professional expertise was on the line. Two recollections here. One is of an inspector that we all rather liked. He was a tall man; Mr May was his name. He always wore a three-piece brown suit. He would take the class himself, and ask questions, and occasionally tell us jokes. He was no grim ogre to terrorise us. He would open his jacket, and then clasp his hands behind his back, so that his large waistcoated stomach sort of mesmerised us. One day, he had been less than careful in adjusting his dress, so that the buttons of his trousers were completely undone. His shirt was plainly visible to us, and we were just beginning to feel the first seismic shocks of imminent (and disastrous) laughter. However, my father had seen it also, and was in an agony of indecision. Should he tell the totally unaware inspector that he was so embarrassingly on display, or should he pretend to see nothing? Or should he fix the whole classroom with an ominous glare of such basilisk threat and promise of terrible retribution that no-one would make the slightest sound or gesture that anything untoward was afoot. It was a period of simmering tension – the class in the grip of the instinct to shriek with laughter, and the headmaster with all his will-power unleashed on his charges. There was a complete and totally respectful silence. All the time, Inspector May continued with his lesson blissfully unaware. Neither did my father tell him afterwards. Better to remain in total ignorance.

Another small anecdote here – this time from a much earlier era. My grandfather's schooldays, in fact. My mother's father attended Croy school in the closing years of the nineteenth century. He told us of an occasion when he inadvertently brought down disaster upon the headmaster of the school. An inspection was due, and the whole school had been primed for the day. All the responses, the tables learned, the dates rehearsed, and everything ready for the actual inspection. This was not to be carried out by a single inspector as in those days the local landowner and the minister were part of the delegation that would assess the school's progress. It was of vital importance to the headmaster and his staff, as it could actually affect their income and even their jobs. One of the ideas of the headmaster was that the inspection party should be greeted, immediately they entered the main classroom, with a rendition by the pupils of a song called "The Woods of Craigielea". At the precise moment the door was opened, all would rise to their feet and the song, in several parts, would burst forth. A truly impressive opening to what was actually to be a nerve-jangling episode in the lives of all in Croy School. Some time before the inspectors were due, the headmaster remembered that he had left some important book or document at his house, and he sent my grandfather to get it. Off he sped. Just as he was approaching the main door with the item that had been forgotten, he saw the impressive sight of the inspection party in a horse drawn vehicle, drawing up at the school gate. He hurried to beat them. He knocked loudly on the door, and threw it open. Immediately, the whole school who had been programmed with many weeks of practice, rose to their feet, and the first bars of "The Woods of Craigielea" pealed forth – passing over the startled head of my grandfather framed in the doorway. Much laughter, of course and much confusion – all of which coincided with the arrival of the tall, black-garbed minister, the laird and the inspector who all frowned with severe disapproval at the chaos of giggling and disorder that confronted them.

And one other experience with the top brass of education in the fifties – the Director of Education. Then, this post was close to the Deity in importance. Nothing like the aura of those days attaches to it in the modern framework – it is almost impossible to emphasise that enough. This was the one man who could bring a catch to the breath and a dangerous skip to the heart if there was an imminent visit to your school.

In those days, the Director of Education for Inverness-shire was one Doctor MacLean. Actually he was a native of Achiltilbuie on the far west coast, but to hear him speak, that would never have been guessed at. His accents were the fluting accents of the then cultural ascendancy. In other words, he "talked posh".

With this in mind, consider what my father felt one day when he had lifted the large black bakelite telephone which was ringing violently in the hall at the foot of the stairs in the schoolhouse.
"Hello."
"Is that Mr Denoon?"
"Yes. Speaking"
And then there began some request or other that immediately had my father burst out laughing.
"OK. All right, Ian. That's enough. You had me going for a minute there. Go on, get off the line...You're not catching me again with the daft accent." And more laughter.
The proprietor of one of the local garages was Ian Grant, a practical joker. One of his specialities was occasionally speaking to people on the phone in the highly anglicised accents of a local former army officer, Brigadier Prendergast, who lived in the village then. He had done it to my father recently, and caught him out completely.
However, it was not Ian Grant on this occasion, but the real Director of Education himself – bemused to say the least at the response from the headmaster of Fort Augustus Junior Secondary School. Unnecessary to paint the picture of the headmaster in his squirming embarrassment when his gaffe became apparent.

And now – one very last school inspector tale. I referred earlier in another context to a famous character in Inverness in the thirties and forties. He was Willie Michie, and he was the well-loved auctioneer in a local furniture salesroom. His performances when he was auctioning had people flock from all around to pack into the rooms just for the sheer entertainment of his wit and rollicking humour. He was also known for his practical jokes. This one was told me by my father, and illustrates the more innocent times then. Willie had been away from the salesrooms on some expedition into the surrounding countryside to check out on some furniture that was to be up for sale. As he drove along a quiet road, he saw a small school obviously in full teaching mode. He apparently stopped and went up ``to the main front door – introduced himself to the young head teacher in charge as a member of His Majesty's School Inspectorate, and asked to be admitted. He questioned the pupils on various things, spoke to the highly nervous teacher, and then left, after pronouncing himself to be completely satisfied with his "inspection". No harm apparently done, but what an outrageous thing actually to do. Difficult to imagine something like this happening today.

Go East, Young Man

After my spell in Fort Augustus Junior Secondary in the primary department, there came the great winnowing wind of those days – the Qualifying Exam. This was accompanied by the Intelligence Test. The build-up to both of these was pretty horrendous since both parents had their own agenda here. Quite simply, this was that it would be unthinkable for the children of the village schoolhouse to be seen to fail to do well in these very public testings. They need not have feared on any of our accounts, and in my case, the doors were opened wide for me to move on to senior secondary school. Here there was a choice for a pupil moving on from Fort Augustus. To the west was Fort William. I think I can only remember one family that sent its offspring there – the distance alone being the main problem. The most obvious and the nearest suitable school was Glenurquhart Senior Secondary at Drumnadrochit (or "Higher Grade" as it was called then). Since my father had been a pupil there, it might seem clear that this would be the choice for me. Not so. It was my mother who presented the most forceful arguments here. She had been a pupil in Inverness Royal Academy and had always been hugely proud of her experience there. That was the school to which her oldest child would be sent and where he would make his academic mark and from where he would bring back glory to the family.

I have to say here and now, that much as I respect and love my now long-gone parents, I have to say that this choice on my behalf was a quite disastrously wrong one. They were not to know this in the early stages, but it became all too obvious later. I detested my period of attendance in Inverness Royal Academy. There. I've said it. However, I do not blame that august institution in the slightest for this, so to assure the Academy that I am not slighting them or their proud history and amassed traditions, let me say that I do not have the tiniest grain of animosity in my soul towards them. I was the one to blame. I was a total and abysmal misfit there in the early fifties. It was all a matter of scale and location. There was a vast social/cultural chasm between a village a long way from Inverness and the town itself. My home was Fort Augustus then and the thirty-three mile journey along Loch Ness side took an hour and a half in the MacBrayne's bus. That was a long distance in those days when a car was less of a natural adjunct to the average home. Inverness was distant and it was alien. Actually, the daily journey into the Academy for me was, originally, from Drumnadrochit to the town. It is very hard to convey the vastness of the gulf that lay between these two places, only fourteen miles apart. Drumnadrochit, where my grandmother lived and with whom I stayed for a spell, seemed a mere nod from my home. It was familiar; it was friendly; it was small and of a scale that I could recognise. But that familiar country ambience of Drumnadrochit melted swiftly away as the bus travelled the miles to Inverness. It faded away, until around Abriachan, it had all but vanished. And Abriachan was a sort of frontier for the other reason that that was where I had been brought up when my father was the headmaster there. From the foot of Abriachan Brae, there was a sort of limbo. Then there was a subtle change in the atmosphere. Fields seemed no longer to be fields "in the country" as it were. They were now adjuncts to something much bigger that lay ahead, just out of sight. Passengers who were now climbing aboard all seemed to be office workers, more like real townies. The big houses at Dochfour and Dochgarroch that looked haughtily down on us through the trees also seemed to anticipate that other world that was now very close.

And there it was. Around the sweep of the road, down from the Craig Dunain junction. You saw the immense bulk of the old Inverness municipal gasometer, which dwarfed the many small streets that lived in its vast shadow. That gasometer *was* Inverness. I still see it in the mind's eye as the town's most dominant feature, even although it has been gone these many years now.

Tension gripped the throat by now. In about fifteen minutes, the day's stretch of late nineteen-forties Scottish Senior Secondary experience would be getting under way. There was the timetable. When was Latin? Where was Maths? Was the worst of the day over swiftly, or did it lie further ahead in the afternoon? It was always best to get the worst over and done with at the beginning of the day. From Farraline Park to the school usually involved a short-cut through the railway station, along by Falcon Square and the almost mediaeval warren of tiny streets crammed with their warehouses and mysteries, that have long ago been swept aside to make way for the present huge buildings that dominate the commercial heart of Inverness. Then you crossed Eastgate at the foot of Crown Road and climbed the strange little narrow staircase that took you on to Stephen's Brae. Then the last few yards till you came to the school gate. In those days, it faced the top of Stephen's brae.

It was always with a heavy heart I contemplated another day in that, to me, vast sandstone building.

Apart from the imposing appearance and presence of Dr D. J. MacDonald, the Rector, one other figure of authority stands out from these days. This was the School Janitor. He was always in dark navy-blue uniform, with silver buttons, and he had a guardsman's cheese cutter cap with the school badge like a regimental totem fixed to its front. During morning assembly, he would stand at a corner of the main hall, at the back, where he seemed to embody the temporal power of the establishment, while "D.J." represented the spiritual – the overarching ethos of the Royal Academy.

A story told me by my mother now. She had been accepted by the Royal Academy, and was taken in from Tomatin by her mother on the first day. She was to be staying in the hostel where the present municipal offices are on Glenurquhart Road – in the same original building in fact. (Extraordinary is it not, for her to stay in a hostel when her home was really as close as Tomatin?) When they arrived at the imposing building, my grandmother approached a resplendent figure standing near the main entrance and enquired humbly about where they should go and what they should do. She thought that she was addressing the Rector. It was the janitor. Presumably the uniform was even more Ruritanian in those days.

Assembly was held every morning in the Main Hall. The whole school was present on these occasions. Most sat on low benches in the body of the hall, while many others stood on the wide, main stairway at the far end. Staff sat at strategic points around the periphery. All of these were reasonably well-catered-for, except a wretched couple of small groups of first year boys, who, because there was no room for them anywhere else, had to stand at the radiators at the two points directly to the right and to the left of the Rector as he looked down from his raised podium and lectern.

The ritual of these occasions had the whole gathering awaiting the moment when the dark curtain behind the podium was parted by an invisible prefect, allowing the magisterial figure of the Rector to climb slowly into view. It was all so brilliantly stage-managed. It was "D.J."'s custom when he had reached the lectern, to grasp it in firm hands and to let his gaze reach out over the gathered school, then to look down, imperiously, at the two huddled groups of first years immediately below him to his left and right. Now, all who passed through that school during the period of D.J.'s stewardship will testify to the man's immense presence. Small and dapper in physical stature he may have been, but he was, without doubt, a giant among educationalists. The following episode might thus be the more readily appreciated. On this particular morning, he had just climbed the steps and the customary ensuing silence had fallen. The imperious eye had, as usual, swept to the right, and then swung in the direction of the group at our radiator where I was standing somewhere in the middle. There came a sudden gasping sound and a heavy thud from directly behind me. One of our company of outcasts had fainted clean away and was now lying inert on the floor. He was duly gathered up and removed from sight and assembly continued. It was incidents like that that didn't do much to ease the nerves of a quaking country misfit such as I. To me it was evidence that the Rectorial eye had the power to fell a boy at twenty paces.

To the left of the main stairs at the back of the hall was an area of darkness and cloakrooms, while beyond that was the annex that once housed a primary school that was attached to the main Academy building. To the right of those stairs, you went, again passing cloakrooms, through to the Science, Art, Music and Geography departments. As an ex-teacher, I know full well the painfully easy targets that members of the profession make when some smart-alec wants to get a bit of his or her own back after the passage of the years, so I'll refrain from savaging those who helped to warp my life in those days, or hold them up to ridicule. They were in the minority in any case. That wing of the school (like the rest of it) did contain its stark contrasts of liberality and enlightenment on the one hand and of dark repression on the other. And anarchy reigned in at least one sad classroom. Names drift by: "Buckie" (Buchanan. Art); "Sly" – short for "Slybacon" (Cunningham: Geography); "Boosey" (Rogers: Music). He was called that because of Boosey and Hawkes the music publishers. And there were many others including the kindly "Hairy Hugh" and the tiny, but fearsome "Parrot".

The overwhelming feeling I get when remembering these long-ago days is still one of depression. No events spring into the mind that have a cheerful echo about them. I can illustrate this easily. The lunch break and the school canteen ought to be at least one memory that would be easy to glance back at with basic pleasant associations. Yet, whenever it unscrolls in my mind, it is an episode of quite crass silliness on my part that actually unravels instead. How about this for a searing little bit of silliness? The Academy school canteen in those days was a long, low, corrugated-iron-clad building that stood in the grounds of the nearby Crown Primary School. As I recollect, we were taken there in groups, supervised by staff. I can see the ticket-handing-over ceremony at the door and then the Spartan interior with its rudimentary tables and unsteady, long benches. The pupils at one of the tables would serve the whole of the canteen – each table doing it for a day. You just had to sit and wait for your meal to be served at your table. In an attempt to impress a fellow diner (female) I once tried a practical joke. The adjacent table to mine was on serving duty, so no-one was sitting at it. The salt cellar stood there, and beside it was one of the plastic drinking cups that were used for water.
"I'll cover their salt cellar with the cup," I thought. "That way, they'll think it's lost ... Tee Hee ..."
Hilarious.
I leaned across nonchalantly and upended the cup over the salt cellar. The cup was filled to the brim with water.
It cascaded over the cellar, the table; it flowed in a tidal wave on to the floor. No cup had ever held such a volume of water. It was a breached Hoover Dam; Victoria Falls in the rainy season. While this was happening in dreadful slow motion, I looked up, stricken, and saw, rearing up, like the kraken from the deeps, one of the more fearsome of the supervising teachers. She had seen it all. I was transfixed in her cold, pitiless stare. She bore down on me and the rest was predictable, public ignominy.

I only stayed with my grandmother for a fairly short spell at the beginning of my first term in the Academy. Next, I found myself for an even briefer spell in an upper flat overlooking Kingsmills shopping centre near the Crown Primary School. Who my landlady was or even what she looked like I cannot now recall. I pass this shopping centre almost daily still and over the years have occasionally tried to work out which of the houses it was that I stayed in such a long time ago. The only thing I had to hold on to was the sound of the bell in the tower of the Crown School and the fact that that tower was visible from my bedroom window. It is only quite recently that I noticed a window in the wall of the flat above the chemist's shop that faces towards that view. Could that be the window I stared out of desperately – totally miserable to be so far from Fort Augustus and familiar things? Who knows?

The next lodgings for me were on Midmills Road – in the house just across the road from where I sit just now, tapping out these words. It is called St Margaret's and is just over the edge of the Hill, at the foot of MacAndrew's Brae and was owned by a local coal merchant. In those days, it was right out on the outskirts of the town, and was extremely large, imposing and the most unlikely looking place to take in "paying guests" – particularly schoolboys such as I and the two others who also were there. They were the sons of a doctor who was working abroad and who were also pupils in the Academy. Another feature that lent distinction was a huge cypress tree that stood beside it on the roadside. You could see it, black against the sky as you walked back from the Academy, along Midmills Road. (It was cut down in the nineteen eighties because it had become a danger with its violent behaviour during storms.) St Margaret's was a large rambling place, and in those days it stood in the middle of extensive grounds. It was shrouded in woods and had endless rolling lawns, greenhouses bursting with vines and gloomy winding paths. It had a veranda at the front that overlooked the lawns, with heavy pillars supporting the overhang. Style it had in abundance. The fact that this household actually had a butler might indicate just how much. Yes, a butler, and he was actually called James. He was a small, dapper Glaswegian with slicked-back, black hair and small trimmed black moustache. On duty, he wore a short white jacket, sharply-creased black trousers and gleaming black shoes. At table and in his up-front household duties he was everything that you would expect: silent, deferential and efficient. Behind the scenes, though, the real

James would emerge – a wee Glaswegian with "aw ra patter" and the ever-present fag. Jeeves he certainly was not. I remember a particular occasion when, as a great treat, I was taken on a tour of the east wing of this huge house – a part that was only used by the family on "state occasions". I was led along forbidden corridors until I recollect standing on a sort of gallery that looked down into an immense, gloomy room with tall bow windows that had stained glass set around them. There was dark panelling everywhere and chandeliers hung from the ceiling. There were trophies from Africa – shields and spears, and animal skins as well. It is truly odd that from where I am sitting at this very moment, gathering these distant recollections, I can look up and see one of the windows that lets into that very room I have just described. Co-incidence in life has chanced upon us building our present house just across the road from the old, grand-colonial-style place of lodging of my early days in secondary education. But the house is no longer what it was. It is now divided up and its glories have long departed. The grounds have been changed utterly with the many houses that have been built where the gardens and the woods once were – indeed almost all of those trees have now gone. I only have the faintest of urges to see what remains of that Gormenghast interior that James took me through on my whispered grand tour all of those many years ago.

My room, when I was staying in that house, was in a small dark green wooden afterthought to the main building – sort of tacked on to the western gable. This whole annex looked rather out of place, propped up against such a grand house. Like an outside toilet at Holyrood Palace. But it contained my humble bedroom. Immediately outside my window were the first of the dark trees of the forest that seemed to stretch into the far distance. It was a gloomy and ghostly outlook and was not helped by the occasions when the moaning winds would have the random stray branch trail its scaly fingers over the roof and along the thin wall. Down the paths through these woods were various mouldering sheds for gardening equipment. If I ever took a walk down one or other of them, it was almost possible to imagine that I was back in the country again – not in the town. But it didn't work. The subtle differences of the town were a part of the leaves, the trunks of the trees, the bushes – everything.

It was on one of those paths that I was to witness a singularly lunatic prank by one of my fellow lodgers – one that could have had really serious consequences. But, first, a little bit of background. In my bedroom there were two fascinating items that had been carelessly left there by the house owners. One was an old-fashioned, double barrelled shotgun with twin, curly hammers that would strike home with loud satisfying clicks when the triggers were pulled. But by far the more exciting to a gun-obsessed youth of those days was a large, heavy air-rifle which was fully functional – if a little bit rusty. The non-technical will bear with me when I mention that one of its fascinations lay in the mechanism that propelled the pellet through its long barrel. Unlike the conventional air-rifle where the spring was compressed towards the stock, this remarkable gun worked on the Webley air-pistol system. And that will be all the technicalities. At first there was no chance of actually trying out this huge, heavy weapon because there were no pellets for it. Until, that is, one day when I was rummaging in a drawer in some dusty piece of furniture. Here I came across a round tin with a satisfactory heavy rattle when it was shaken. It was a cache of .22 air rifle lead pellets. In a trice, we had sneaked the rifle into the dim and invisible-from-the-house reaches of the woods and had quickly established the fact that it had considerable power and would have leaping tin cans peppered with ragged holes. Then it was that my fellow lodger had one of those red mists come over his eyes and normal behaviour and judgements were put aside. As is the nature of our species. We had only about three or four pellets left, and found ourselves crouching down at the fence that separated us from the garden of the large house next door. The elderly gardener who worked there was moving around between the flowerbeds and going about his normal drudgery. He bent over to pull some weeds or something, and presented us with a standard target that my companion found it impossible to resist. At first when I saw the barrel of the air-rifle aiming in his direction, I took it to be make-believe. Not so. The heavy thump of the release of the spring said otherwise. I turned in terror and fled blundering back to the house. I was propelled by this terror of guilt by association into the gloom of my room in the lean-to and its imagined safety. Now I have to say that it is very doubtful if the pellet actually struck home. The range was too far and no memory exists of the huge retribution that would have been visited upon us for such an act of hooliganism and folly. It was not long after this that I left this house and moved to very different lodgings in Innes Street. Before I leave for the totally different world I was about to enter, a final word about the House on the Hill. All of the extended family who lived there in the late forties have gone or will have died. I completely lost touch with them all after I had left. I can still conjure up a flitting memory of James, the butler, standing silent in his white jacket – dapper as a thirties screen idol. I can see the rest of us around the table with the French windows in the background: my landlady, an elderly uncle, and the various young people: the son and daughter of the house and the other two "paying guests". All of us are waiting for the master of the house – the coal merchant – to enter. He appears, bald-headed, affable, tweeded and plus-foured. He sits down at the head of the table and that is the signal for the grace to be sung. Yes, sung! The final two lines were:

"Thank You for the birds that sing,
Thank you, Lord, for everything...."

It certainly was an extraordinary place for a country cousin to spend a portion of his life at an impressionable age.

In The Shadow of the gasworks

The switch to 36 Innes Street at the other side of the town was a quantum leap on the social scale. My new lodgings stood in the lee of the old town gasworks, and with the main railway line to the north immediately to the rear. The contrast could not have been more total and stunning. I don't think I was particularly aware of class in those days, but I did realise that I had been moved from an atmosphere of domestic spaciousness and privilege; from among strangers of several generations who were originally pretty alien to me, though who soon proved to be kindly. Suddenly my world shrank to a single room in a narrow working-class street that was to be my home for more than a year and a half. From this immense distance, I can't recollect that aspect having made a huge dent on my consciousness. I can only assume that it was the always-looming dread of the school I was attending that blotted out all such considerations.

My landlady in Number 36 Innes Street was Mrs Cameron. She lives on in my memory as someone a little bit like Ma Broon. Always in her wrap-around patterned apron and with her hair drawn back in a bun. She was kindly and I was indeed well-looked after in my room. And there was the nub of the problem with Number 36. I lived in that room exclusively while lodging there. I didn't take any meals with the rest of the household. I have a notion that Mr Cameron was an invalid, and never left the house. I do know that I never actually saw more than a solitary glimpse, through a partly open door, of a hunched shape, smoking a pipe, in a chair by the fireside. There was a son of the house whom I did occasionally see and speak to; I think he worked on the railway. However, my memory is strangely vague about many of the details of life there. It was the overwhelming effect of that dark room. The bed was a large couch that Mrs Cameron folded down every night for me, arranging the sheets and the bedspread. There was a heavy table against the wall by the window that also had a leaf that folded down for meals or for the inevitable dreary homework. I can remember a cabinet that had various ornaments in it – in particular, a scaled down model of a German helmet with Nazi symbols on it.

Why didn't they ask me to join them at meal-times? It would have made such a huge difference to life then. But it was never suggested or expected. I do remember that Mrs Cameron's chips were especially marvellous. They were the best I had ever tasted. I asked her how she got them to be so consistently brown and firm.

"Simple," she said. "Just add some salt to the fat and they'll always come out brown like that."

Here I am all those many years later and I've never actually tried to see if this really works. It's getting a bit late to try now.

The lighting in the dark-wallpapered room was supplied by gas. It is difficult to conjure up nowadays what it was like to have lighting that was so dim that you had to huddle close up in order to read. Whether it was the single gas mantle, the hissing Tilley lamp or the silent, elegant Aladdin. The fire in the room was one of those pipe-clay, honey-comb-columned gas ones as well. Between the light and the gas fire, there was a lot of hissing in that room during the winter evenings.

Then there was the other essential room. The lavatory. The one at Number 36 was of the outside variety, and it was an ever-present threat to peace of mind. To get to it, you had to go down the narrow, inky-black stairs. Then you had to feel your way along an equally inky, narrow corridor till you felt the outline of the back door that let you out into the small yard, just under the railway. There was no light to help you and the experience was utterly terrifying. Every grisly image from "Tales of the Supernatural" (there was a large volume with that title back home that I had long ago read) came rushing back into my cringing consciousness as I was feeling my way along these cold sinister walls. Getting there was bad enough but there was then always the return journey, which could be just as hellish. It never seemed to have dawned on me that a torch might be a good idea. One thing was certain: the more primitive bodily functions adapted to fit in with the threat of these ghastly journeys. Sometimes the awful experience would be further added to by the shattering noise of the passing trains on the Inverness to Wick line that was literally at the foot of the garden. The whole street seemed to shake when these monsters crashed past.

There was also persistent noise from the other direction as well. This came from the Inverness Gas Works. There was a continuous crashing from the hopper and its endless chain of buckets that lifted the coal into the gas-processing plant. The gasometer towered over Innes Street. How many today can remember that huge, grey landmark with its mysterious gallery of windows at the top of its louvered outer skin? It was the town's most dominant feature. I can still see it in the mind's eye as the first bit of Inverness to come into view as the bus from the west swept down the last brae from the Craig Dunain road-end. I managed to get a last photograph of it some years ago, on the very day it was beginning to be demolished. The odd-looking "penthouse" feature at the top had already disappeared and the tiny insect-workmen were busy unpicking its rivets and joints and removing its grey carapace. The whole huge thing seemed to vanish overnight without comment or farewell from the town it had stood over and dominated for so long.

The window of my room in Number 36 Innes Street overlooked the street. It was the usual jutting-out variety and allowed fairly generous sweep of view. To my left, I could see up to the block that held number 21 where she lived. Yes – SHE – the object of my hopeless yearnings. She was in my class in first year but never after that, because I slid remorselessly down the academic slope from then on. Longings were unrequited, since she was pledged to my pal of those days - Johnny Fraser from Abban Street.

Just a few years back, I revisited Number 36. I stood outside it and looked up at that window. The building seemed relatively unchanged on that occasion over the nearly fifty years that had elapsed. The window itself still hadn't succumbed to the glib sales talk of the double-glazing man, though the metal spike atop the pointed front had gone. It all looked so compressed and tiny as it always does on such occasions. One memory did come rushing back to me though. In spite of the presence in Number 21 up the street, it was in the other direction that I spent most of my time staring hopelessly. This was in the general direction of Loch Ness and the Great Glen and in particular the far western end of the Loch where Fort Augustus and my home lay. Every week was the steady countdown till Friday and the bus back there for the weekend.

When I think of Innes Street now, the prevailing impression is of darkness. Yes, there was the noise and the smell: the gasworks to the one side and the railway line to the other with the pounding locomotives shouldering their way up the incline towards the vanished Joseph Mitchell Bridge that the floods of 1989 so spectacularly swept away. The street itself was lit by gas lamps of the old traditional kind so that the light they gave was rather fitful.

They were spread quite far apart, so that each one stood in its own little island of light until the next lamp was approached. One extraordinary sight was the regular appearance of the ancient steam lorry that used to thresh and churn its way up the street from the gasworks to somewhere or other with loads of by-products of the gas manufacturing process. It was quite a bizarre sight. Smoke belched from the thin funnel that stuck out of the cab roof and the furious noise of its chain-driven transmission echoed down the street. How the driver managed to keep its furnace stoked up and keep an eye on the road at the same time? There was no-one in the cab with him as I recollect. Then what an inferno it must have been inside that cab on even a mild summer's day.

And the final memory is one of a near-escape for me. It was firework time. I had my own bangers on this occasion – ones that gave me some amount of kudos among the others in the street. They were small aluminium tubes, sealed at one end and each had a fuse of tarred twine that had a gunpowder core. The bang these tiny things made was quite shattering when compared with even the most powerful that were available in those days. Anyone who knows about these things will know that I am describing the detonators that were used for firing gelignite. So, how did I get hold of such items? Remember, these were the days of vast upheavals in the Highlands. Hydro-electric schemes, dams, tunnels and huge armies of navvies in their vast camps were changing the physical face of my world. High explosives were basic to all of this, and to say that security was lax in the matter of looking after all this deadly ordnance was an understatement. Some of my pals from my home village had little difficulty in getting into a storage shed that had been left unlocked and had helped themselves. Detonators were handed out freely. I got my share too.

None of us had the remotest idea of how volatile these were and it is nothing short of miraculous that there were no appalling injuries from things that I was later told could even go off with the heat of the hand. But in Innes Street, I knew nothing of this, and strutted around with my super bangers, which one by one sent out their shock waves rolling along the length of the street. Until, that is, an adult loomed from the darkness.

"Who's letting off these bangers?"

We all looked at him.

"How do you mean? It's just bangers ..."

"No, it bloody well isn't! I know the noise of detonators. Come on. Which one of you is it?"

The walls were closing in. There was still one left in my pocket. What if he searched me? The clang of prison doors reverberated. But all was well; the interrogation faded away and the threatening adult retreated into his house with nothing more ominous than: "Just watch out, you lot ..."

That was the end of the detonators, needless to say

The Bridge Street Bogey Man

Now, I cannot leave these memories of my far-from-happy school days in Inverness from 1949 to 1952/3 without going back a few years to an episode that dates from an earlier era – probably before the family moved from Abriachan to Fort Augustus.

First of all, the location. Generations now walk the streets of Inverness who know nothing of what the town centre looked like before the brutish insensitivity of the nineteen fifties and sixties planners and architects was let loose – as it was in so many other towns and cities throughout the land in that unhappy design era. You can still stare at the leprous concrete boxes that house the Inverness Museum above the windswept emptiness of Upper Bridge Street (a slum from the day it was created) and you can still be astonished that such a design could pass the checks and counter-checks of committees of local people who knew and loved their town, and ever be allowed to see the light of day. But at the appointed hour, and in the face of many cries of outrage, the iron weights swung on the ends of the cables, suspended from the jibs of the huge cranes, and down in clouds of dust tumbled Old Bridge Street with its solid rows of shops and cafes, above which venerable houses had looked down on the world that passed below. There had been narrow closes that opened out into court-yards behind, with winding stone steps leading up to the doors of these houses. One of these had a plaque that told of Robert Burns having stayed there during his famous tour of the Highlands. Down it crashed as well. And at the foot of that street, there was the enormous castellated buttress of the eastern end of the most eccentric suspension bridge that ever spanned an unsuspecting river. From the Bridge Street end, the huge cables swooped from a structure that looked like a Norman keep, yet the western end had the cables rise over small humps of masonry before silently disappearing into the ground. What a tourist magnet all of that would have been today.

I knew this long-lost world so well, because in one of those houses in the Old Bridge Street, lived my Aunt Teenie (stress the "ee" to give it the real old Inverness flavour) with her extended family. She was the sister of my grandmother from Drumnadrochit (my father's mother), and I would often call in to see her when I was attending the Academy. I even remember going there in trepidation once to borrow my bus fare so that I could go home for the weekend to Fort Augustus. Do people like Auntie Teenie still exist? She was a quite extraordinary presence. She was large and bulking and was always dressed in black. She had her own chair, set back-centre of the kitchen/living room. You immediately felt her warmth the moment you entered the room and her accent was the quintessence of the Inverness accent of old. It was slow; it flattened the vowels; it was kindly to the point of ridiculousness. There always seemed to be an endless procession of visitors, each one being offered the inevitable cup of tea. This was provided by her daughter Chrissie, who presided over the cooker that received its gas from a huge meter that took a single penny at a time. There always seemed to be a frantic hunt for pennies as the cooker – and the gas fire – began to sigh and flicker. Alec and Johnny were her two sons. Alec was almost totally silent, while brother Johnny, the barber, was the talkative one. The room was dark and mysterious. Corners never seemed to yield up their secrets and ornaments and mementoes littered every surface and cupboard and mantelpiece. I can still see the golf ball held by its three little silver clubs on to its plinth. Johnny had scored a hole-in-one with it, the tiny silver plaque told the world. The rest of the house was even more mysterious – except for the toilet. It was truly a thing of amazement. It was across a small landing, and was housed in a sort of overhang over the courtyard. You could actually see the grey flagstones far below you through a gap in the floorboards. The pedestal was quite enormous and of bizarre design. On the wall opposite hung a picture. I think it was of Gladstone. He stared glassily ahead. The rest of this intriguing house was approached along a dark corridor. Again, I have to use that overused word "mysterious", though this time qualified by "utterly" because I was never allowed to visit there. Until one day, and I cannot remember why, Alec, the silent one, took me through and into the room that overlooked Bridge Street. My overwhelming impression is of darkness. Victorian draperies hung at the windows and heavy furniture crouched all around. The windows looked right out over the narrow street, and it seemed to me that I could almost have leaned out and touched the roofs of the buses as they rumbled past.

I think you'll have the picture, so now to the Bogey Man. He actually comes from the period in my life when I was young enough to have my parents being frightened about me or my brother and sister, wandering down through the close and into the unknown dangers of Bridge Street. "You mustn't ever go down there," an adult had solemnly told us. "If you do, the Bogey Man will catch you and take you away in his barrow."

We believed this, of course, and took care that if we did go down the stone steps towards the courtyard, we would not even let our feet touch the actual flagstones unless a parent was accompanying us.

Then that incredible day when we actually SAW him. The Bogey Man.

His face was white as chalk. He was thin and stooping. He wore dark overalls or a coat of some kind. But most terrifying of all, he was pushing in front of him an enormous black hand-cart with silent, rubber tyres. He moved across the courtyard, opened a grey, windowless door and disappeared inside with the cart. We watched in silent horror. He emerged after a short while, locked the door, and moved back silently past the foot of the stairs where we were sitting frozen in disbelief and then vanished down the close and out into the street. We stared at each other, quite terrified. So there WAS a real Bogey Man and the adults had not been lying. He was waiting to get us if we ever disobeyed. And so it was that every visit we made to Auntie Teenie's after that, we would sit on the stone stairs – dread clutching us – waiting to hear the soft rush of the wheels, and see the dark sinister shape with the dead-white face, heading towards the place where he kept his grisly hand-cart. What children had he collected that day in his hand-cart, and what was their fate behind the grey door?

It was not till some time later that I found out that the Bogey Man was an employee of a nearby bakery, and used the hand cart to make deliveries. Little did he guess the stark terror that he instilled in us as he went about his daily innocent business.

I could still wish that there actually had been such a thing as the Bogey Man – a real one – who could have been around when those crass people in the fifties and sixties were destroying such a wonderful street as the original Bridge Street had been. Whatever the fate that awaited them in his lair would have been too good for them.

Fred J Kelly's

On Union Street in Inverness, there is a branch of a well-known chain of wine stores. Behind the cheerful advertisements for the latest wine bargain from Chile or California, the front has a sort of old-fashioned look about it. These are the premises that once bore the name of Fred J. Kelly. To me this name still means the shop where the best possible of gents' clothing could be obtained. This was truly **the** gents' outfitters of the North. But it was also more than that to me in my Academy days – and in later years too.

My father had been a regular customer there for many years and when it came to me getting kitted out for my spell in the Royal Academy, it was to Kelly's we unquestioningly went for the blazer and the scarf – and not forgetting the cap. This was the kind that schoolboys in the "Wizard", the "Hotspur" and the "Rover" wore. They moulded to the heads of Inverness schoolboys in those days too. Not every boy wore one as I recollect, but they did exist. I don't really remember if I wore it all that often. But back to Kelly's. It did not have the sole rights regarding the selling of the Royal Academy regalia. Shand and Lindsay's and Cameron's also sold the blue blazer and the blue and yellow, broad, horizontally-striped woollen scarf as well. They may have done so, but it was Kelly's version that had the more precise shade of blue and the correct intensity of gold. But even more important – the badge on the blazers of those other two establishments was bought separately and sewn on while Kelly's was embroidered directly on to the breast pocket of the garment. It was a Rolls Royce job, so it was there that I was taken to have me made, at least, to look like an Academy scholar.

Fred J Kelly's was a temple to sartorial maleness. The interior panelling was dark – not too dark, but of a discreet mellow wood. There were racks of open-fronted drawers filled with shirts; there were stands with hats and caps and there were the masses of socks and ties. Under the glass counter, were the presentation boxes of cuff-links and other of the more decorative aspects of male attire. And the air was permeated with the scent of new cloth. I can recollect the assistants there too and some names linger on over the years. There was Fred J. himself, father of two sons, Robin and Fred – who took over management in the fifties. He was a tall, military-looking figure who, my father told me, was an expert marksman and who had competed at Bisley. The assistants were all turned out impeccably of course but not in a dandified fashion. Just the correct statement, almost understatement, with not a fold or crease that could draw a critical glance. My father knew them all and the greetings flew around whenever he entered the shop. One was tall and elegant and a keen fisherman. I remember him as Hossack. Just his second name. I can recall the numbing effect on me of the news that he had been drowned in an accident somewhere north when fishing in a river in Caithness. People like him were too secure in their hold on life for such things to happen to them. Then there was Jimmy Chisholm. He was smaller – even portly – and always seemed to sport a tan. An always-cheerful, dapper figure. He, I was told, had been a piper in a Scottish regiment in the Western Desert campaign during the war. I even heard that his pipes had been blown away by a close-bursting shell during the siege of Tobruk.

To get fitted out with a jacket or trousers, you went downstairs to the basement, past the pictures of soldiers in the scarlet tunics of long-ago regiments. Precisely the sort of theme you would expect on such walls. The ritual of choosing from the huge choice on the rails along the walls and in the display cabinets was a lengthy one and the changing room with its firmly shut door and frightening all round mirrors was the last staging post before the choice was made. Always a time of agonising indecision. When I heard in the eighties that Kelly's was being threatened with being sold, it was quite impossible to take seriously. Of all local businesses, it seemed the most secure and established. The sense of sheer disbelief when the first rumours emerged is still with me but it was all too quickly confirmed by the next visit. It was even more shocking when a letter arrived informing me that my outstanding account had to be paid forthwith. It was only then that I realised another of the advantages of being a long-standing customer of Fred J Kelly's – their delightfully vague and informal "Budget Account" system that allowed the purchase of one expensive item a year, and having it wrapped up and taken from the shop without the sordid business of passing grubby bank notes across the counter or even a cheque. Just a modest sum per month or per banker's order. How civilised. How Fred J Kelly.

In one small sense, Fred J Kelly has not gone entirely. When next you are in that wine store for your medicinal pick-me-up, just glance down at the threshold. On the step you will still see, inscribed in mosaic, the name of the gents' outfitters that brought lustre to the towns of Inverness – and not to forget – Elgin.

Good old Fred J Kelly – gone but decidedly not forgotten.

NICKED

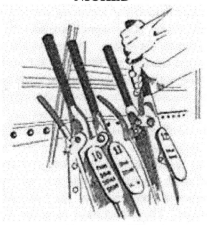

And now for a final scrap of Academy days angst - and this will be the very last. The occasion when I picked up a criminal record. When I was staying in Innes Street, one of my regular dates was with the signalman on the north railway line. Let me explain. I was friendly with a boy from Abban Street, Johnny Fraser, who was fanatical about locomotives and all to do with railways. I was also keen on that sort of thing, but not with quite his level of commitment and detailed knowledge. Somehow of other, he had made contact with this particular signalman who I remember as being rather elderly, and presumably near retirement. Whatever his status, he was more than a little careless in his interpretation of the rules and regulations of his profession, since I am pretty sure that they did not permit him to have regular visits from schoolboys when he was on duty. Whatever his motive, we were privy to the excitements and mysteries of the railway signalling system in full action. At first we were only able to watch, but there were occasions when one or other of us would be allowed to pull one of the immense steel levers to raise or lower a distant signal. These were operated by cables that ran alongside the railway track, on guiding pulley wheels. There was one signal, visible from the box, at the point where the line swept across the river on the old stone bridge built by the great Highland railway engineer of the nineteenth century, Joseph Mitchell, that I was allowed to activate. Because it was relatively closer, there was not quite the same amount of energy required to work it. It was

really gratifying to see the distant arm raise as if in salute some seconds after you had hauled the gleaming steel handle towards you and had it lock into place. This signal box was truly a very special place to be in on a winter's evening. There was a coal fire glowing in the dimness, the wind beating on the glass and the various moving lights of the railway traffic out there in the darkness, with all their attendant noise and smoke and the lights of the signals winking in the distance in the murk outside. We came to understand the complicated and no-doubt now-extinct mysteries of the tablet systems with their attendant accompanying bell codes that were exchanged between the signalmen and were in place to prevent two trains entering the same stretch of single line in opposite directions. One of the highlights of each visit was the fish and chips that came from a works canteen. They must have been the best fish and chips in the whole of the North of Scotland. However, this small world of pretty innocent rule-breaking was to come to a rather spectacular end for me and Johnny. We were heading back to Innes Street one night, when we were intercepted by a couple of members of the Railway Police. In those days, they still wore the tall helmets that had been abandoned by most of the Scottish force, so they had a sort of alien look about them. Our names were taken and we were delivered a ferocious lecture about the perils of trespassing on railway property. We didn't dare to mention that we had been for most of the evening in the nearby signal box, helping to haul the levers. We were aware that the signal man could have been in trouble. Pretty shaken, we made for home. The shock of this unpleasant encounter was eased by the fact that the holidays were almost upon us. After the holidays, when I got back to Number 36 Innes Street, Mrs Cameron, my landlady asked, "Did you get the summons, then?"
Silence.
The sort of stillness when the very sky turns red.
"What summons?"
"The summons for you to go to court. I told them your home address and they said that it would be delivered there."
I cannot recollect a more anguished period of tension during that period of my life. Every day, I waited for the wrathful response from Fort Augustus and to have the very heavens crash down upon me. But nothing ever came. As for Johnny, he had to make his appearance in some court and was fined for trespassing. As for me –

nothing. That dreaded summons never made its appearance. It must have fallen down behind a filing cabinet somewhere. I suppose I'm safe enough by now.

But that will have to be all about Inverness Academy. As I have said on more than one occasion, it was a particularly stressful and miserable time of my early life. No room to reflect on the Academy prefects of those days with their god-like presences – and the sure and certain knowledge that their "gold braid and epaulettes" would never be for the likes of me. Or to dwell too much on that awful day when the official assessment of my future educational prospects was laid on the Rectorial desk before the stunned gaze of my parents: "A practical education, not an academic one, would be in his best interests."

Just room enough left for me to say that the Academy didn't get it right every time. Thank God for that.

The Glenurquhart Experience

The shock of the move from Inverness Academy to Glenurquhart Senior Secondary was pretty profound. Apart from the fact that Glenurquhart School was so very much smaller, there was the additional problem of my name being so well-known there in advance. The headmaster, Alistair C MacKell, was a much-respected local character (apart from his schoolmasterly duties he was also prominent in many community activities as well as being a local historian) and was a second cousin of my father, the headmaster of Fort Augustus Junior Secondary. As well as that, one or other of the teachers who were local also knew about me and my family. My own grandmother was also a well-known local figure and lived in her small house at the back of Victoria Buildings behind the grocer's shop. So there was nowhere for me to hide. It was already known, of course, that I had been rather ignominiously ejected from the Academy – not for wrong-doing or villainy or anything exciting like that - but just for ineptitude at schoolwork. I remember graphically to this day, my very first encounter with a truly fearsome member of the Glenurquhart staff. She was Chrissie MacDonald. Her nickname to all who encountered her was "Chrissie Croik". I can only assume that the nickname meant that there was some family connection with the small community of that name that has such indelible associations with the Highland Clearances. Anyway, once encountered, never forgotten. I had just taken my seat in the classroom – she taught French – and was aware that she had fixed me with her pale terrifying eyes. Then, in a voice that had the chill of death: "Well, my lad, I hope you don't think you're going to bring any of your fancy ways with you into my classroom. I think you'll find I have my own way of dealing with them." And the sycophantic sniggers of a truly cowed class followed directly. All stared, of course.

However, it is with Alastair C MacKell, the headmaster that I will have to dwell a little longer in order to illustrate just how much the spirit of a school was affected by the kind of person who is in charge. Certainly in those days, the stamp was firm and absolute. The whole tone of the place: the atmosphere, its ethos – all were overwhelmingly dictated by the towering presence of this man. He had joined the staff in the early thirties and when the then headmaster, Fraser (the "Broch"), retired. A. C. MacKell had succeeded him. It seems that in many ways he modelled himself on the Broch, who also had been a fierce and domineering figure. And so it was that he too ruled with an absolute sternness. As I have mentioned, he was a second cousin of my father's, but no hint of this family connection ever tempered or modified his dealings with either me or my brother or sister. That was not in the character of the man. He was tall – or certainly seemed to be so – in that he always held himself stiffly erect while he paced along in his characteristic slow and measured fashion. The shoulders were held back, his waistcoat was thrust out in front and his hands were clasped behind his back. His head was quite small and narrow, and his colour was high. His hair was still dark and close-cropped. He always wore the same three-piece suit, which seemed to be one size too small, of a small, herring-bone, grey-flecked tweed – all of the foregoing rising out of a pair of polished black boots. But it is his voice that all who passed through Glenurquhart School will remember for ever. It was quite high-pitched and came from the back of the throat. It was also a bit nasal. It was so distinctive and, as a consequence, so easy to mimic, that any gathering of former pupils of that era will lapse into "Ally MacKell" if ever they should meet. Even to this day. He also made a strange sort of catarrhal clicking sound from somewhere deep in his sinus passages which would punctuate his speech and this too was a joy for the lampooner. You cannot really describe it - but we all mimicked him. You just couldn't help it. Jacky MacDonald from Milton was probably the best of my era. On more than one occasion that I can remember he would place a hand high on the outside of a classroom door – when there was an unsupervised racket going on inside – so that you could just see the fingers curling round on the inside and, with the reedy voice trembling the rafters and the sinus clicking and spitting, he would fling the door wide to find us cowering in a sudden paralysis of terror.

In his hip pocket, Ally MacKell carried The Belt. It was leather, it was black; it was fairly broad and was folded once, in the middle. An unwary wrong-doer might look up from his misdemeanour to see the tall, grey-suited angel of retribution bearing down upon him, hand already reaching to the back pocket and sweeping the belt into the air in one swift, fluid action – the air already vibrating to, "Out with

your hand, boy!" and all followed instantly by the sharp crack of
Scottish traditional discipline being administered.

And we accepted it all. It is at this point that you enter difficult
waters when looking back at these values. Ally MacKell was, overall,
a popular and much respected headmaster for all his ruthlessness. He
could never have behaved as he did in later decades when referrals,
exclusions (then later, inclusions) and a myriad checks and child-
centred methods took the place of the summary punishments of those
days. He moved in completely different times with values far
removed from those of today. Our lives then were adumbrated by the
constant threat of corporal punishment. A. C. MacKell set the
standard for Glenurquhart Secondary School and the rest of the staff
followed his example and guidance with their own varying degrees of
ruthlessness. In spite of that, we didn't fear it all that much from Ally
himself. There was a kind of primitive sportsmanship about it and a
general lack of real malice. You were caught: it was a fair cop and
indeed a sort of crude chalking-up of beltings received and totting-up
of scores for competitive purposes sometimes took place. The
belting for inadequate work - the failure to learn by heart some
passage of prose or piece of poetry – was automatic. It was just an
integral part of the education framework. The actual belt he used, the
flat black one, was not as villainous a weapon as the vicious thong of
the Lochgelly "Extra" which was used by most of the others. That
was indeed an evil thing, and hurt badly. Ally's chosen implement
would explode like a sharp clap of thunder, cause a brief rush of pain,
but did not cripple the nervous system. And, like thunder, it was
mainly a startling, unwelcome, occasionally frightening thing. It was
just a part of the natural order and scheme of things. We were indeed
privileged to have come under the influence of such a man of
learning and stature. But the darker side of it all was the constant fear
along with the almost intolerable burden of remorseless homework.
This latter seemed only to exaggerate in the mind the complexities of
the subjects being learned so that the prospect of the insurmountable
Himalayas of the final examinations presented a vast and insuperable
obstacle. As a teacher he was impressive – especially when it was
his favourite subject: English. While working with a relatively small
group of senior pupils, his love of language and ideas would
communicate instantly and many owe him a great debt that
contemporary teaching methods might find it hard to match. He was

a teacher in the traditional sense of that word: we sat and listened – and were taught. There was humour too. When a man of such gravitas indulged in verbal horseplay on occasion, it would make a particularly powerful impression. And another powerful impression was that left by his occasional fierce forays into bringing even sterner discipline into the running of his school. One fixation he had was that the "Bus People" (theme to be developed later) were tardy in their morning walk from the bus stop down to the actual school. After we had got off the bus at the Bradley Martin Hall, he would watch for us along the quarter mile stretch of road from one of the tall gable windows. If he considered that our steps were not smart enough or that we were wilfully dallying, then he would explode into action. It would take the form of his appearance at the narrow entrance gate, usually with the belt in his hand. The reedy voice would announce at top pitch that "last one past me will get the belt" and for us to hurry as if our lives depended upon it. Suddenly our fifties gabardine coats flapped, boots pounded and canvas knapsacks leaped on our backs as we elbowed and fought to avoid the hand reaching out to pluck the last boy (never a girl) who ran gasping past him. Then the sweep and crack as the threat was duly carried out. Somebody's day would have begun in spectacular Glenurquhart style.

And a final thought here that is prompted by the notion of A C MacKell's influence on Glenurquhart Secondary School in those days. It is that most of the memories I have of then seem to be fixed in a winter frame. Why should this be? Perhaps because these were the grimmest days. For starters there was the pervading, gnawing cold. Numbness spread upwards from the chilled feet through the whole body. I can still see the sudden view of Glen Urquhart that you get when you round the corner above Urquhart Castle at Strone. It is an ordered glen, with its villages, farms and crofts spread below and up on to the hillsides. Normally this is a beautiful view, but it was most decidedly not so to our eyes in those days. To us, in the centre of that broad sweep of glen, lay the School. Not visible yet among its surrounding trees, but, above it in those harsh winter days, there always seemed to be wreaths of cold mist, still and menacing. Frost always seemed to linger for a longer spell down there, away from the comforting rays of the sun. And when that view did come into view, there was yet another significance: only about ten minutes remained for us to scramble through the final tattered shreds of copied homework before we shuffled reluctantly out of the bus, and hunched silently down the road towards the tall, gothic windows – bracing ourselves inwardly for whatever Ally MacKell and the school could hurl at us.

The Bus People and the Homework Blight

I have already referred to the "Bus People". This term, with its echoes of prehistoric man (the Beaker People) was the one used to describe the large group of pupils who travelled to Glenurquhart School in the nineteen fifties from the west – from Fort Augustus and all places between. It was a term that carried with it more than a slight tone of condescension in the minds of some (but not all) of the Glen staff. We felt that we were looked at as rather a shifty lot and not up to the standards of the native Glen youth.

The run from Fort Augustus to Drumnadrochit is approximately nineteen miles, so that it meant an unnaturally early start to the school day for us. The buses that transported us were MacBrayne's, and around them grew a whole subculture and way of life. A kind of camaraderie arose between us and most of our drivers – though there was open war with some of them. The most outstanding of these drivers were Sandy MacDonald ("Sandack") from Fort Augustus and Jocky Grant from Invermoriston. Sandack was probably the most methodical, disciplined and reliable driver who ever piloted a bus along Loch Ness side. No digital watch of our times could ever match the nanosecond timing of Sandack's stately progress in the old Commer bus with its three-speed gearbox, its tall roof, its rudimentary low-backed seats and its sliding door at the front with its long, chromium handle. It winter it was miserably cold with its totally useless heater-grille down at the far-distant front of the vehicle and with its windows rimed with remorseless frost. Probably the most irritating feature of the Commer bus was the low-backed seats because it allowed Sandack to have a clear sweep of the whole of the bus in his rear-view mirror. One of our adolescent cravings then was smoking. Many of us were addicted. A day when there wasn't even a five-pack of Woodbines between us was the most depressing of all. It was as if we needed the fix of nicotine to dull the senses against the grim day that lay ahead In Glenurquhart Senior Secondary School. The other driver in the mornings was the already-mentioned Jocky Grant. He was a very different character from Sandack. While the latter – though kindly and well enough liked by us – always had a hint of the stern church-elder adult about him, Jocky on the other hand, was small, rotund and rubicund of complexion. His driving style was more flamboyant and the solemn pacing through the gears was not Jocky's style at all. And he could join in the general banter with us – but, best of all, he would turn a Nelsonian eye when the fags were being lit up.

The bus run home in the evening, after the day in school, was very different. We hadn't any idea from week to week which driver we might have on these occasions. It must have been a rather unpopular watch for each of these drivers. You can imagine his feelings as he headed through the village of Drumnadrochit with a light scattering of passengers sitting peacefully behind him, and then rounding the final corner heading towards the stop at the Bradley Martin Memorial Hall. Straight ahead of him he would see the seething mass of the just-released inmates of one of the most repressive educational establishments in the Highlands, all staring in his direction and heaving and jostling to get into his bus first. Quite an unpleasant sight we must have been. And I have to say that we did tend to blow off some of the head of steam of our pent-up repressions. Various of the drivers would react in different ways. Some would bellow at us and order us to sit down and shut up. Moderate success there – sometimes. There was always the ultimate threat that some caught on to, of reporting us to the headmaster, Ally MacKell. That could be pretty effective. We weren't all that nice a lot either, I have to say, and there was more than an element of intellectual arrogance in our attitudes. After all, we were being transported – the intellectual cream of our home villages – to a neighbouring community for our secondary education. I remember howls of laughter greeting one driver's frenzied admonition to us after he had slammed on the brakes. Her leapt to his feet and glared at us. "I'm no having any more of this bloody hirality (sic) in my bus .....!!"

But the other total obsession during these bus journeys was one that occurred in the morning runs. That thing was Homework. Now I had had the experience of another secondary school – Inverness Royal Academy – before coming to Drumnadrochit. I knew full well the burden of homework laid on the shoulders of secondary pupils in those days. Nothing, however, could have prepared me for the Glenurquhart Secondary School Experience. Homework here was quite unbelievable. The numbers of books we had to transport in order to do this homework meant that we all had to have enormous bags in which to carry them. The boys – and some of the girls – had ex-service knapsacks (not haversacks: they were too small) sagging from their backs. I actually still have mine mouldering at the bottom of a cupboard. It was an ex-RAF knapsack and it not only carried the straining weight of the mildewed, monstrous Victorian tomes during the school session, it also carried my piece box and flask during the many holiday jobs that were available in those days. I suspect that the philosophy behind Glenurquhart School's homework policy was really quite simple. Freedom (actually not being in school, that is) equalled frivolity and unproductiveness, in Calvinistic terms. Such time must be filled to the very brim with French and Latin vocabulary, reams of historical dates and Corn Laws and Metternichs and Bismarks; endless theorems to be committed to memory; algebra, solid geometry (the only kind of advanced maths I could ever do for some reason); trigonometry and so on and so on. But worse, by far, than all of the foregoing was the special purgatory of the Weekend Essay. Each Friday afternoon, the title of this abomination would be handed out by the English teacher and the dissertation (nothing light or superficial would ever be accepted) had to be handed in first thing on the Monday morning. No exceptions or no excuses. And the thunderbolts of wrath and retribution if you hadn't done it would be instant and fearsome. The most futile excuse of the Bus People was along the lines of "I did do it, but I left it on the bus". This was curtly brushed aside as an apostasy as unforgivable as you had admitted you hadn't done it because you couldn't be bothered. You might think that with the three evenings that the weekend provided, there would be plenty of time to get the essay and all the other stuff done. Not so. You have to take into account another remorseless force of those days: the power of The Sabbath. Actually, ours wasn't a very committed sabbatarian household, but there were residual traces of it in the air. This took the form of "no homework on Sunday". So if you hadn't got the hideous burden dealt with in the Friday and the Saturday, then anything else had to be done covertly on the Sunday. It had to be done in the manner of a resistance fighter with secret radio, under cover of almost-darkness and with look-outs posted. At the sound of an approaching parent, exercise books would be swept from sight, and something more spiritual would be substituted.

But that essay truly blighted each and every weekend. Even those of us who were lucky to be more fluent with words loathed it with a deep loathing. Probably it was inflicted upon us (apart from the Calvinist element) so that we would become more skilled at expressing ourselves on paper. But many must have been put off the idea of committing their thoughts to paper for the rest of their lives. What was all the more infuriating and frustrating about this homework regime was that you knew the various departments didn't communicate with each other. English demanded the many-paged essay – a monstrous task in itself – but Maths, French, Latin and the rest all piled on their own share of the misery as well. The hunched backs of the Glen pupils from the west – the Bus People – bowed under their tonnage of books on a Friday evening as they trudged up the road towards the bus stop, reflected the mixed feelings of that moment: joy at being free for the weekend, but tempered by the grim prospect of the gargantuan labours that lay ahead.

On most mornings, during the bus journey to school, most of us would be bent over books, either trying to learn a slab of Geoffrey Chaucer (we were made to learn by heart almost the whole of the Prologue To The Canterbury Tales. Have a glance at it one day, and reflect upon its length and the manner of language in which it is written.) or else a portion of the Old Testament for Bible Study, or doing Maths exercises or French, or whatever. It was only that very few of our number who actually were able to cope with the demands placed upon us by the system who would be able to look out at the passing landscape as we proceeded on our way along Loch Ness side. Their only concern would be for the safety of their own exercise books, which would be circulating so that the rest of us could copy down feverishly as much as we could of their weekend labours. So selfless indeed. These paragons were essential to our survival and they were perfectly willing to allow us to benefit from their greater diligence and wisdom. The genius at mathematics might board the bus at Invermoriston. From there, there would be more than enough time left of the journey to shift the contents of his exercise book into your own. But what if it was the Latin home exercise that hadn't been done? Duncan MacDonald came on at Primrose Bay quite a bit further down the road, leaving you quite a bit less time to affect the transfer. Then there was the ever-present, appalling prospect of one of these vitally important individuals being absent on the very day when he or she was most needed. The hollow cry:"He's not there …!" would ring out with all the despair of the damned in the deepest pit of Hell.

And we learned special skills on these fraught journeys too. Often you might have to stand for most of the way. The ability to write reasonably legibly in an ink exercise book while the bus swayed and surged on its soggy springs was one that had to be developed. Then there were the tricks that were employed in times of especial crisis. This one was told to me long after the event; I was unaware of it at the time, so it could have occurred after I had left Glenurquhart School. This is how it went. Rhona, the daughter of Ronald Guthrie the bank manager in Fort Augustus, had an air of placid innocence about her and always wore a navy-blue coat with a hood on it during the winter. She had a pale, round face and was known when she was younger, in her first year, to have a tendency towards travel sickness. This was seized upon one day when it became clear that the frantic homework copiers were not going to make it in time. Drumnadrochit was getting dangerously close and there were only about two more stops ahead. Someone said to her: "Go on. Pretend you're sick. Tell Sandack and he'll have to stop." She pulled a lugubrious sick expression on to her normally white features and stumbled to the front of the bus with her hand held ominously up to her mouth. She tapped Sandack on the shoulder. When he turned and saw her livid face, now with both hands clasped to her mouth and ominous gulping sounds already close to his ear, he slammed on the brakes to let her off – fast. She stayed outside of the bus for several minutes, making all the appropriate sounds, till the frenzied rush of mad scribbling had managed to get the bulk of the trickiest stuff copied safely into exercise books. She got a signal from inside, and slowly climbed back on board. Obviously this one couldn't be used too often as it would soon be rumbled by Sandack, but I was told that it was employed on more than one occasion when things were especially dire. Such was the desperation that the homework regime in Glenurquhart School could bring about in those days.

Final thought on the homework. I have wondered about the fierce discipline of the Glen school in those days and how it could have affected our behaviour patterns in various ways. A memory of one of our more violent playground games springs to mind. This one was particularly vicious and took place in winter time, when there was snow on the ground. This was for the boys in our segregated areas. The bulk of us would line up with hard, soaking-wet snowballs - whirled round fiercely to get surplus water out of them to make them even harder –and certain individuals would run, one at a time, at headlong speed down the length of the outside corrugated iron wall of the science building, while the rest of us unleashed our torrent of rock-hard projectiles, trying to hit them. The thunder of the mass of dangerously hard snowballs crashing against the metal wall was a satisfying noise to us. All the better if you managed to score a direct hit. I am sure that we were working something out of our systems at the unrelenting sternness of that school.

Epic Belting of Fifty Two

A road-side monument stands above Loch Ness, at Lenie, in the form of a seven-foot cairn, to the Great Belting of Fifty Two. The bronze plaque set into the monument tells us that this event occurred on September 29th, 1952.

Actually, the inscription on that plaque tells the passer-by that the main reason for the monument being erected there is to commemorate the death on that day of John Cobb who was killed when his jet speed boat disintegrated at over two hundred miles per hour on the loch, opposite that point. He had been attempting to gain the world water speed record. The Great Belting was a parallel event that lay behind the main drama of that day – a small one by comparison – but one that had its own unique epic qualities.

The fierce disciplinary code of Glenurquhart Secondary School meant that truancy was a rare event. The fact that one of the most spectacularly amazing dramas of those years was unfolding on our very doorsteps was a huge source of excitement and pride. However, the other fact that all of John Cobb's trial runs on the loch were carried out during the day when we were all at school and therefore could not witness them, was a source of bitter frustration. But on one glorious occasion, we did make a dramatic gesture – and "we" refers to the fatally flawed "Bus People". I am sure that all us who made that rash, insane choice on that far-off September morning will have the sequel burned deep into our psyches for the rest of our days.

For a spell of several weeks during that magical autumn of 1952, Glenurquhart had been at the front line of the world's media eyes. Film crews and hordes of photographers and reporters had arrived to witness the breaking of the world water speed record by the most unlikely-looking of heroes: John Cobb. Unlikely, in that he looked for all the world like an elderly, bulky and benign bank manager; also in that he showed uncharacteristic thoughtfulness for a visiting Englishman in refraining from any record-breaking activities on Sundays, to avoid ruffling local sabbatarianism which was still strong in those days. The whole atmosphere was drenched in the excitement of it all. It was the sharp end of nineteen-fifties high-tech. These were the days when you might see the gentle drift of a De Havilland Rapide biplane along the length of Loch Ness. Now, daily, the scream of the De Havilland "Ghost" jet engine mounted in the beautiful silver and red speed boat with its slender, tapering prow and its two huge stabilising sponsons, pierced even into the dark, insulated world of Chrissie Croik's French classroom. It thrilled our senses and snatched our attention away from regular verbs and the vendettas of old Corsica, and had us wonder feverishly if there was going to be an attempt on the record that day.

How to convey the frustration? Our daily bus runs in the morning and in the evening were both geared precisely to miss the stupendous event when it took place – or even any of the many practice runs that John Cobb made in "Crusader" along the measured mile at Lenie, less than a mile from Urquhart Castle. One morning we heard the shriek of the engine near Primrose Bay when Crusader was turning before hurtling back eastwards again. But dense trees effectively blocked out the loch at that point and it was futile to ask Sandack the driver to let us off to try to have a look. On another occasion I recollect that as we were rounding the headland just above Urquhart Castle, we saw Crusader in the distance, being towed back to its base at Temple Pier. But apart from that, not a single glimpse of Crusader in action were we able to get.

There was one occasion, though, when I was included in two coach-loads of folk from Glenmoriston who were being taken to Rosemarkie on a day trip, organised by the minister at Invermoriston, Reverend Peter Fraser. (And why was I, a native of Fort Augustus, one of that party? I was there by special invitation of the Rev Peter himself to be the on-board entertainer on the bus for the older trippers. I was a noted performer on the mouth organ at concerts in those days, though I must confess that the temptations of the bus with the younger trippers were too strong for me.) The minister had asked John Cobb in advance if it would be all right if the buses were to stop at Temple Pier to have a look at Crusader and even maybe to have a few words from the Great Man himself. With one of those gestures that had John Cobb referred to on his memorial as a "gallant *gentleman*", he agreed to this and we all duly lined up at the tape stretched across to hold us back from approaching too close to the speedboat. It was on its trailer in the converted shed with the shining aluminium doors. Cobb, a tall, bulky man, in cloth cap and suit then appeared and spoke to us quietly and afterwards answered various questions. It was really remarkable that he would have done this, in the middle of his vastly expensive expedition with its tight schedules.

I still have a photograph that someone took of him when he was talking to us that day, looking just a little bit like Jacques Tati the French comedian in profile, and with me, a round-faced youth, among the throng in front of him.

And now – a mystery. All my life, since these now-distant days, I have held a memory of a weekend stay at my grandmother's at Victoria Buildings in Drumnadrochit. One afternoon, my brother and I had set off to walk the mile or so to Temple Pier to have an unofficial close-up look at Crusader. This was possible because Gordon Menzies who actually lived at Temple Pier was in my brother's class at the Glen School. I see in the mind's eye, sharply etched, the beautiful speedboat on its trailer; the name Vospers (builders of Crusader) on the side, and my amazement on seeing the tiny rudder that actually steered the craft. All this being taken in at leisure as we walked round the trailer. Before committing this to the page, though, I thought that I'd better check up with my brother on some of the finer details. He told me that the event never took place. He had never seen Crusader close-up and I had to be imagining the whole episode. Maybe so, but the memory remains just as vivid in spite of his disclaimer. I know I was there – but who was it with me?

The wait for a suitable day for the record attempt – dead calm surface on the loch – became almost unbearable for us. Until, on the morning of September the 29th, when our school bus with the thirty-plus pupils aboard approached the long stretch of road that overlooked John Cobb's measured mile at Lenie. Someone called out," Look. The timekeeper's boat's in place. He's going to try for the record!"

And sure enough, out on the smooth loch surface, the craft was sitting motionless. On board were the official timekeepers whose task it was to measure the speed of the jet speedboat as it made its two runs – first from the east past Urquhart Castle, and the return in the opposite direction. Many cars and lorries had stopped all along the roadside and were drawn up on the verges. People were standing about, leaning on the fence. All were staring to the east from where Crusader would make its appearance, under full throttle to hurtle past our eyes on the way to where it would turn around to repeat the performance, its jet engine echoing off the dark hills, before claiming the world water speed record. None of us there had the tiniest doubt that John Cobb would be successful. All of us on the bus were gripped by the prospect of what was just about to unfold. We were all at the right hand side of the bus craning to see as much as we could through the windows.

I genuinely do not remember whose idea it originally was. In whose mind the shocking idea of mass truancy first germinated. I have more than a fancy that it could have been I. We had been so tantalisingly close to these events for the past few amazing weeks, yet only had managed to catch the occasional fleeting glimpse worth mentioning. Now the main event was about to take place before the massed cameras and journalists of the world – and we were going to miss it all yet again. Not this time we weren't! Sandack did try to make us see sense; to realise the enormity of what we were now doing, but he had no chance. The majority of us (a few timid souls didn't join us) tumbled out of the bus with our bulging schoolbags, and joined the rest of the expectant crowds lining the roadside. Almost thirty pupils of Glenurquhart Secondary School had rebelled. We were filled with a mixture of exultation and dread at what we had just done. We watched the back of the departing MacBrayne's bus, aware that the die was cast and that there was now no turning back. But it would all be so worth it.

Well, we waited and we waited. Then came the first hint that the vile perversity of the weather was going to foul up everything yet again. The dark smoothness of the loch surface was beginning to break up into ripples as an increasingly strong breeze swept over it. After some time, we saw that the timekeeper's boat was moving from its station. It was clear that the attempt was now off. Our mad gesture had all been in vain. The driver of the next service bus was amazed at the sight of the now cowed army standing in a despondent huddle by the roadside, waving him to stop. There was little conversation as we hunched aboard. All the bravado had evaporated. A dull certainty of awful impending events was building up in us. We headed silently down the long straight road from the stop at the Bradley Martin Memorial, towards the grim Gothic windows set in the school gable. There was still no sign of A. C. MacKell. He must have been on the lookout for the mutineers, his fury simmering. Then he was there. It was truly appalling. This was no act: he really was incensed at the scale of this mass truancy. His face was the deep purple we knew was the distillation of purest rage. We stood sullenly in the gale of his bellowing wrath. There was no possible excuse. Our sin was clear and it was unambiguous and after we were lined up alongside the corrugated iron wall of the science building, MacKell strode along the line of cringing humanity and belted the lot of us. All the boys, that is. By that odd chivalric code that prevailed in those days, any girls who had joined us in our rebellion would have been exempt. We were shaken and appalled by the ferocity of it all, but in the context of those days, it was no more or less than we had expected and we were able to cope. A strange ritual dance: we had our parts to play and our responses to make.

We returned to our classrooms where we got more haranguing. All prejudices against the lack or moral fibre of the Bus People were confirmed.

Later that day, when we were bent over our desks, we heard the distant scream of the De Havilland "Ghost". He was going to make his attempt after all. Then some time later, a member of staff came in and whispered something to our teacher. A pause. Then we were told that there had been an accident on the loch. Crusader had crashed and was destroyed. John Cobb, however, had survived. We were struck dumb. This was not in the script. Our belief in the invincibility of the technology of the day; of shining, beautiful machines and of quiet men in white engineers' overalls – how could all of these let us down? Some time soon after, the news came through that John Cobb had been killed instantly his speedboat had disintegrated. His corpse had been dragged from the water and propped up in a boat, so that watchers from the shore had initially thought that he had survived.

So far as I am aware, only one cine-camera tracked John Cobb's last fatal run. It was filmed through a telephoto lens, but the quality of picture that has survived is poor. It does show the hunched shoulders of the engine casing of the beautiful craft which gave it its special, dynamic, ahead-of-its-time purposeful appearance. It flings out the welter of boiling spray behind it as it lances the echoing V of the hills of the Glen. Its frame vibrates in reaction to the surface of the water; then the vibration becomes a sudden catastrophic rocking motion that buries the nose of Crusader, catapulting the heavy rear completely over. Something can be seen being flung clear and ploughing a churning furrow far ahead. This appears to be the body of the doomed pilot.

On the way home from school that evening, I got out of the bus with a pal, Jimmy Innes from Invermoriston, and we slithered down the steep hillside to the loch shore far below. We wanted to see if there were any scraps of Crusader washed up. We didn't think there was anything ghoulish about this. The beautiful silver and red craft had been an icon to us. We were not able to comprehend that it had been destroyed so utterly and on such a public stage. The search for a small scrap of it seemed a perfectly natural thing to be doing. There was nothing to be found of course. However, my brother later got, from classmate Gordon Menzies, a couple of scraps of the remnants of the funeral pyre of pieces of Crusader that had been burned by the shattered and distraught Cobb team at Temple Pier. There was a shred of plywood and a solitary aluminium bolt, fused and blackened from the fire. I still have them. This momentous September episode all those years ago did teach us one sobering lesson. We had it brought home forcibly that our human species is so pitifully fallible. Nothing could have looked more confident and set for triumph as that great Loch Ness Expedition of Nineteen Fifty Two – from the breath-taking appearance of Crusader with its attendant white-garbed engineers – to the quiet bulk of John Cobb, the leader, himself. None of us harboured the tiniest shred of doubt about the outcome of it all. Then, in an instant violent boiling of the loch's surface, it was all snuffed out forever. As for the ferocious retribution dealt out to us for our act of gloriously defiant truancy – it might be a cause for wonder for later generations that we so docilely accepted such crude methods of discipline in those days.

Clash of Cultures

The opening sentence of the prologue to L.P Hartley's novel, "The Go-Between" goes as follows. *"The past is a foreign country: they do things differently there."* It has a mellow resonance to it, but the truth it contains is even more startling when you consider events in your own life-time: events that still seem close enough in your memory to be reached out to and touched. One such for me was a cringingly awful Saturday morning when I had organised a team of local boys from Fort Augustus to take the bus to Drumnadrochit to make total and utter fools of ourselves in a manner that will appear absurd to the younger reader today. These were the days before television had made its way across the hills to enlighten us about the ways of the great big world out there. This has to be borne in mind as this tale unfolds. A true tale.

The game that we played in both Fort Augustus and Drumnadrochit was shinty. My father encouraged it and organised it in his own school and all of us spent much of our time practising and honing our skills with club and ball. In the Glen school, several of us made it into the school team and took part – reasonably successfully – in the various contests of those days. Shinty was the only sport that we knew how to play and whose rules we fully understood.

One day, we heard that a new and energetic young minister had arrived in Drumnadrochit. He noticed the local youth playing their strange, native game and decided (as incomers often tend to do) that they required some civilised values introduced and, being a keen footballer, he soon had a youth team up and running. Those of us not from the Glen heard all about this in a neutral sort of way. After all, we knew what football was and often would punt one around among ourselves whenever we got the chance. Then came the day when the challenge was issued. I was asked by some of the Glen footballers if I could get a team together from Fort Augustus one Saturday and come to Blairbeg pitch at Drum for a match. No bother, I said and easily got the necessary volunteers. I asked my father if I could borrow a set of jerseys and shorts from Fort Augustus School, and he lent us the strip from the Market Hill team – it consisted of a red top with navy shorts. Or it may have been the green and white of Bunoich. The grimness of what happened that day has erased such minor details from my mind. So it was that we all foregathered on the appointed morning and off we headed to Drumnadrochit on the early bus – not any more concerned than any other group of players anywhere else who were heading off to a contest of skills. I do have to say, however, that at this early stage we were already missing one vital piece of equipment. Our shinty clubs. We felt incomplete.

We changed into our strips in the village hall at Blairbeg and soon we were clattering in our lumpy fifties football boots, across the road to the field where the long, low football goals and the strange pitch markings were awaiting us. There was a small crowd of locals lining the pitch, watching the Glen players as they practised headers and the rest. To complete this sense of serious organisation on the part of the Glen, there was also a referee in regulation black uniform. Now a distinct chill of unease began to settle over me, and – I suspect – several of the rest of the Fort Augustus group too. All we had meant to do was to meet a similar number of our Glen pals and have a kick-around for an hour and a bit and then get Sandack's bus back home in time for our tea. There had never been any idea that it would all turn out to be something as formal as this. But worse – very much worse – was to follow in an ever-increasing spiral of humiliation. The first real crack appeared in the sky when the referee asked for the captain of the Fort Augustus team to step forward. There actually wasn't one, but since I had organised it from that end, I vaguely owned up.

He looked at me.

"What do you think you're up to? Did you think nobody would have counted?

"Counted what?" I asked, bemused.

"Your players. You've got twelve."

"What's wrong with that?" (Everyone knew there were twelve players in a team. A shinty team, that is.)

Pause.

"Well, there should be eleven."

"Oh, my God!"

One of our most expendable was immediately sent to the touchline.

The whistle shrilled and we were all summoned to the centre of the field to get the usual exhortation about gentlemanly behaviour and the rest. By now, the sense of nakedness brought on by the lack of a shinty club in our hands was quite distressing. We felt totally and utterly vulnerable.

But now the real madness was about to be unleashed. As soon as the ref had finished his little speech, most of the Fort Augustus team headed immediately to their places on the field. The way you do in shinty. Forwards ran forward and the backs moved back.

As a full-forward, I ran up the field and stood beside the opposing full-back, greeting him cheerfully. He was gaping at me. The ref by now had understood and the small crowd were now hugging themselves – laughing at the hayseeds from the west who were by now really making their day for them. Again the referee's whistle dragged us back to the centre of the pitch.

"Do you lot actually know the rules of football? Any of you?" he asked incredulously.

We looked at each other.

"Well, no. Not actually."

There followed a brief lesson on the basics and the game got started at last. No need to tell you what the outcome was. A grim thrashing for Fort Augustus.

I said at the outset of this tale that all of these things took place in the pre-TV days of the early fifties. Up until then, I had never seen a complete football match – in fact I would never have seen one at all. Neither had any of my companions from the village - certainly none of the wretched group who shuffled ignominiously back to the village hall to get changed afterwards: aching to get as far away as possible from the laughter of the Glen spectators and the whole miserable debacle. Yes, we would see on the screen when the Highlands and Islands Film Guild van called at the village hall at home, excerpts of matches being played in far-away places, but this was not enough to tell you the offside rules of football – or even how a game actually got under way.

A foreign country indeed. Mind you, I have to say that in spite of the vast amount of football that TV provides nowadays, I still do not have the faintest idea about the offside rules of that game. It is still the classical simplicity of the shinty offside rule that immediately springs to mind.

Victoria Buildings

At the foot of the stairs in our house in Inverness, hangs a large photograph of a remarkably attractive young woman. She has the style and graceful clothing of the Edwardian years preceding the First World War. The photograph seems to have been meant to look as if it had been taken out of doors, with the subject standing in front of a doorway framed with a dense growth if ivy. She has a wide-brimmed, flat-crowned straw hat with ribbons, hanging from her left hand. Her sleeves are wide and the light-coloured dress, which could be white, is full and sweeps the ground. A black belt encircles her narrow waist. Her high-necked blouse has a single string of large pearls round it. The final detail that gives away the precise era is her hair, piled up as it is in the exact fashion of the "Gibson Girl" look. The photograph carries the name "Charles Treasurer, 21 Inglis Street, Inverness" in elaborate scroll at the foot of the frame. Treasurer, the photographer, had apparently used this image for many years, presumably among others, to advertise his business. This would explain the heavy, expensive frame in which is mounted. When his business finally ended, the picture was gifted to the subject. The subject was my grandmother – my father's mother – who has now been dead since 1974.

There are a few small clues in that photograph as to when it had been taken. There is a wedding ring on the appropriate finger, so that means that by then she was Margaret Denoon and no longer Margaret Maclean from Braefield in Glenurquhart. I have always found the circumstances of that marriage interesting. The name "Denoon" has come to me (via my grandmother and father) from Denoon the Chemists, a once well-known business in Inverness. My grandmother's husband's parents who owned this business both died young: he, Robert Denoon, in 1878, aged 31 and she, Mary Anne Munro, in 1884. My grandfather was brought up by his uncle, Dan Munro and his wife in Shewglie House, Glenurquhart. Donald Andrew Denoon (my grandfather) had been left a considerable sum of money by his wealthy parents for his upbringing. He attended Corriemonie School while my grandmother attended Balnain School. When my grandmother and Donald Denoon eventually met and decided to get married, his uncle and aunt were highly disapproving since my grandmother, coming from a humble crofting background, was deemed not to be a suitable match for someone being brought up in the grandeur of Shewglie House. As is frequently the case in such matters, all such objections were futile and married they were in 1905. They moved into Inverness and lived in a house in Bellfield Park where my father was born. Next, with the help of the money left him by his parents, Donald Denoon bought a small shop in Maryburgh. However he was continually dogged by bad health and they were forced to sell up the business and return to Glen Urquhart. My grandmother's family home was empty at this time and she and her family moved into Braefield. It was here, on January 2nd 1913 that my grandfather died of tuberculosis at the age of 36. My grandmother stayed on at Braefield until her brother Tom came back from the War – as did her sister Annie who had been working on munitions.

Her next move was to the village of Lewiston where she and her two sons, Robert the elder and Donnie, lived in a house, which was part of the Lewiston Arms Hotel. They stayed on there until after my father had left Glenurquhart Secondary School. There was a new owner of the hotel who had plans for development, so there had to be another move – this time to Douglas Row, down by the river, in Inverness. This was only of a very short duration and in 1928 she moved back to Drumnadrochit and took up residence in the small house at the back of Victoria Buildings. So to return to the photograph briefly – it must have been taken shortly after she married, and because she is wearing light-coloured clothes, the date was certainly before 1913. As was the custom in her era, a widow wore black from the day of bereavement, as did my grandmother, for the rest of her life. I cannot pass Victoria Buildings (overlooking the sharp left-hand turn – heading west - of the main road in Drumnadrochit before it sweeps across the sloping bridge over the River Endrick) without seeing her in the mind's eye. Not as the beauty in the Charles Treasurer photograph, but as the small, strong-willed and much-loved grandmotherly presence in our family's life from my earliest dimmest memories up until the end of her life in 1974 at the age of ninety seven. Within that span of years, she scarcely seemed to change except for the inevitable failings towards the final months she spent in Victoria Buildings. She possessed that dangerously deceptive quality of permanence in our lives. We could never conceive of her not being there. Nothing changed inside the house either. Except for the mighty cast-iron range that used to dominate her living room. My father and uncle got together to have its immense and basically inefficient bulk heaved out, to be replaced first by a conventional fire, and later by an electric one. It may have been a kindness to my grandmother but it did remove something that seemed to reflect her own character and beliefs. Like her Calvinist faith it demanded great sacrifice and unremitting effort to keep its small but intense fire glowing brightly in the grate. The briefest spell of inattention and it might fade.

Actually arriving at her house had its own special sort of minor drama. The narrow, dark passageway to the left of the present shop front is still there and when you come to the end of it, the tiny two-storey house that was hers is still there also. It looks eerily much the same at first glance as if the more than thirty years since she last lived there had never been. But it is now completely renovated after various spells of being used as a store and dwelling place. It is currently a chic-looking bijou residence with amenities that my grandmother could not even have imagined.

A visit to her began with the opening of the wobbly wooden gate into her tiny, packed garden and twisting the mechanical bell device on her front door. Then you entered the small wooden outside lobby with pots of flowers (geraniums mainly) and plants on shelves on either side, filling the tiny windows. Next, into the equally diminutive hallway. The floor always creaked in theatrical fashion beside the coat and hat-stand that had a dully-glaring, stuffed cormorant standing incongruously on the floor under it. (This had been shot by my father when he was headmaster at Elgol in Skye.) All visitors, once this far in, assumed the rest and the loosely rattling doorknob on the living room door was the final confirmation for my grandmother that visitors had arrived and that it was stroopack time. In latter years, the visitor would usually find her sitting by the fire, reading or toasting her speciality – oatcakes – but in earlier, more agile times, she could be cutting sticks at the gable of the house or be somewhere up the steep flight of steps (still visible today) that my uncle had constructed for her to have access to her large garden on the upper level, overlooking the Victoria Buildings complex. This garden provided vegetables, flowers as well as rasps and apples in season. On one occasion we were startled to hear her disembodied voice from somewhere above us as the gate was being pushed open.

There she was – at the very top of the looming, ivy-clad wall that all of her front windows stared directly into. She was busy picking rasps or brambles and hanging precariously over the twelve to fifteen feet drop to the path below. On this particular occasion she would have been in her late seventies.

A family visit to her in the nineteen fifties was an experience that had its ups and downs. The meals that we sat down to were definitely a plus. We sat around the bulk of the heavy table on high-backed, green velvet, moquette-upholstered chairs. It could have been for her rabbit pie with its unique, crunchy short pastry lid or any of the other specialities that we had come to look forward to. Afterwards there were the vast, wild woods that climbed up the hill beyond the fence at the back of the upper garden. These were a marvellous adventure ground – in fact, Drumnadrochit as a village to be explored always provided comparison and contrast with our own Fort Augustus. And all the time, there was the anticipated return to the narrow, dark close and the small house at the back of Leslie's shop lying ahead, and whatever there was to be for supper.

But the visit to Victoria Buildings wasn't all childhood idyll. I've already mentioned my grandmother's Calvinism. My parents did live their lives by a mild sabbatarian code and a certain lip service was paid to Lord's Day Observance. It wasn't too oppressive – more a source of mild irritation than anything else. But at my grandmother's, it was the Real Thing. Even the puckering of the lips in preparation for a small tune was enough to draw a rebuke. Never a sharp or declamatory rebuke though – just a sad shaking of the head and a sense being conveyed of her deep sadness at the pain being experienced by Our Lord at such a thoughtless act on my part. Reading of anything other than the Good Book just was not on. But the biggest turn-off was the occasional attendance at church. This was in the Free Church at the nearby village of Milton. Not the present modest building that now stands there but the larger and much more severe one that stood there before being consumed by fire in 1954. Memories of the interior of this church are more like the apocalyptic etchings of Gustav Doré. Vast Gloom; dark drapes and a pulpit so high that the minister looked like Moses on his pinnacle of rock, arms outstretched to part the Red Sea. Frequently it was for the Gaelic services that I was obliged to accompany her: as a non-Gaelic speaker, this was an especial ordeal.

My grandmother on her tall, Victorian bicycle was a regular sight on the roads between Drumnadrochit and the neighbouring villages of Milton or Lewiston. She kept this solid dignified machine in the large shed behind Victoria Buildings where firewood was stored along with various gardening tools and things. It had the gauze guard over the rear wheel that was required in Victorian or Edwardian times to keep the full billowing skirts of the female cyclists from getting caught up in the spinning spokes. Towards the end of her more active life, however, my father and uncle became a little concerned about their octogenarian mother hurtling down the steep slope of the bridge across the River Endrick on the main road, if she was pedalling her away across to Lewiston to visit someone or other. The tale had got back to one or other of the brothers that she had been spied one evening after lighting-up time, by the local policemen, on just such a mission. The small, black-garbed figure came swishing down the road past the police station with not a light, front or rear, in evidence. The bobby stepped out and signalled her to stop, calling out her name. She waved cheerily back to him, merely greeting him with something like, "And good evening to you, 'bronian'," before disappearing into the gathering gloom. It was my uncle who took matters into his own hands. After telling my grandmother that her bicycling days were now over, he made doubly certain by hoisting the great bike up and tying it to the rafters of the shed, well out of her reach. It presumably stayed there until that shed was eventually demolished.

My grandmother also had a sort of mystical quality about her. It was something that could bring that frisson of being in the presence of the unknown and the second sight. I became aware of it first on an occasion when we had arrived at her door one Saturday afternoon on a spur-of-the-moment family visit. Instead of looking surprised when we opened the door into her living room, all she said was: "I thought you'd have been earlier. But I've made some oatcakes for your tea." It was during the run home in the car up the lochside that one of us addressed the question: "What did she mean 'I expected you'd have been earlier'?" My father then told us that his mother often dreamed that we would be visiting her the night before the actual visit. She would sometimes announce it by saying, "I saw you standing at the end of my bed last night, and you said that you'd be calling by." It didn't happen all the time, of course, but often enough for it to have quite a profound effect on me and my brother and sister.

I had a personal experience of this during the final months she lived at Victoria Buildings. I'd been to see her to do some job or other for her – probably in her garden – and had noticed that she wasn't her usual self. She had been looking frailer of late, but I got the usual cup of tea and we had the usual blether. I drove off back to Inverness. I was home for about an hour, when I felt an overwhelming urge to get into the car and to drive back to Drumnadrochit. I could not fully understand it. She had not been anything more than a little more quiet than usual. Nothing serious. It was when I emerged from the close beside the shop and was approaching her small gate that I saw her outline and her pale face at her upstairs bedroom window. Never before had I ever seen her on the lookout like that. It seemed that just after I had left to go back to Inverness, her electricity had failed. The next-door neighbours were away from home so she was left with the grim prospect of no heat or light. By this time she was virtually housebound, so could not contemplate looking further afield for help. "I prayed for you to come back and help." She told me. "I knew that you would come." I did come back, and was able to see to the fuses or whatever had been the problem. Presumably it had just been a whim on my part to make that journey back to her house, but it did seem to tie up with her strange prescience in these matters.

She now lies buried in one of the older parts of the strangely atmospheric Tomnachurich cemetery – the part where the headstones all have the lush ornamentation of a bygone age. The large red stone carries the details of her parents-in-law, her husband and herself. The enormous gap in years between her husband's death and her own reminds that she spent the vastly greater part of her long life as a widow. Because the dead in this part of the cemetery have no further link with the living, the well-kept grass lacks the punctuation of the splashes of colour of flowers left in their memory. Except for one, of course. During a very recent visit, I reached down as I always do into the dense closely-trimmed bush standing close by, to check that the ancient lemonade bottle was still there. It was the one that she used to carry water for the flowers she regularly left in memory of her husband. Yes, it was still there. I then found myself stretching even further down. I always remembered that she kept a gardening glove there as well – a heavy canvas one with thick rubber coating. Amazingly, I found myself drawing it out into the light for the first time in over three decades. There it was, only the red of the covering rubber had now faded to a ghostly white.

Apart from that recent sudden compressing of the years, there is another way in which she continues to make her presence felt in my daily life. The central feature of her living room was a splendid pendulum clock. It had been manufactured by the Ansonia Clock Company of New York. I inherited it when her last possessions were being shared out. On its face are my father's initials (R.A.D.) and my Uncle Donnie's (D.E.D.) Mine can also be seen faintly with the date 1952. This clock had ticked away all of her adult life – or even all of her life. I had once been told that it had actually been her parents' clock. It has been ticking away in our house since 1974 (except for a very expensive visit to a clockmaker over twelve years ago) and it still has pride of place on the sideboard across from me where I now sit as I am reading and editing this. If the passing of the hours during a sleepless night has to be punctuated, then what better way than by those same slow, mellow chimes that once drifted up the narrow staircase, along the cramped little landing and into my grandmother's guest bedroom in the house tucked away at the back of Victoria Buildings in Drumnadrochit all those many years ago.

The Labourer – and the Worthiness of his Hire

Forestry Days

My generation has had to absorb and adapt itself to many social revolutions over the years and to learn many harsh lessons. Attitudes and values taken for granted have been questioned and scrutinised by cold eyes and have been cast aside. In the area of employment this has been particularly so, and the right of all members of a society to have access to a job that will provide for life is more now of a luxury for the few than the birthright of all. The sneer at the concept of "a job for life" is a familiar one in the political dialogue of our present times. All of which leads me, rather loosely, to the next theme I wish to address.

As I mentioned earlier, in my school and student days, holiday jobs of a bewildering variety were available in or around my home village of Fort Augustus. Apart from the interest and excitement some of them provided, there was the joy of relative financial independence for a part of the year at least. The invaluable training for life that they provided I have already alluded to and is too obvious to dwell upon. From the age of thirteen or fourteen to twenty one, I worked in the Forestry Commission, I worked as a truck driver, as a ghillie on a shooting estate, as a worker in a fruit-canning factory in Norfolk, as a driver of a grocery van, a labourer in a saw-mill, as labourer on road-building projects, as shopkeeper in a Hydro-electric workers' camp and as a postie on various occasions. And that is only a part of the picture. Forestry, for example, covers a whole range of different jobs from the felling of standing timber to the tedious weeding in the vast open-air nurseries that were used then. In the retailing industry, I did about the lot at different times.

But it is with the Forestry that I'll start.

In the middle of the Great Glen, we were surrounded by it. It dominated our lives up till the coming of the Hydro-Electric schemes. The hills around us were carpeted with the regular rectangles of dark green conifers so detested by environmentalists today. To us, they were quite natural. Many local men and women worked in the Forestry. Scarcely a day passed without us being reminded of it. There were the dull green lorries on the roads and the groups of Forestry workers from the village who tramped up the brae past our house, heading towards Auchterawe and the seedling nurseries. These workers were male and female, though sometimes it could be hard to tell at first glance – all were dressed in the most shapeless of shabby garments – suitable for the basic, hard outdoor work they were expected to do. It was all so much a part of the fabric of the village that I still look on myself as an old Forestry hand. My experiences in it covered the years from the very early fifties right up to the end of that decade. I and many of my contemporaries worked in the Forestry Commission during summer, Easter and even Christmas school holidays – and later during the university holidays. The pay was reasonable though not extravagant.

Then, the Commission had a sort of timelessness about it. After all, what is more primal than the forests themselves – even man-created ones?

There was also a strong military feeling about it too. This was brought about by its internal structure. The highest-ranking officer was the remote and permanently invisible Conservator – equivalent to a general or field marshal. The high-ranking staff officers then in descending order: the Divisional Officers (Colonels or Majors); District Officers (Lieutenants); Foresters (Regimental Sergeant Majors); Foremen (Sergeants); Gangers (Corporals). Then you came to the actual workers in the squads - equivalent to the poor bloody infantry. When we worked there as school pupils I suppose we were part of an even more humble category. The only parallel might be the Orientals who were drafted in to the front during the First World War to dig the trenches. Or maybe that's taking it a bit far.

Then the garb of the Forestry workers. For the main part it was ex-army. The tunics, trousers and coats were almost all ex-forces. The only actual Forestry Commission garb that could be termed a uniform was that worn by the Foresters. It was a green tweed jacket with a russet collar and a crown insignia. The bag for the "piece" was invariably a haversack or a back pack of heavy military canvas. This piece bag was about the most important item that we carried. To the casual passer by it might seem that nothing was more delicate and infinitely precious than this. They were handled as if they were delicate traceries of finest Meissen china-ware. If you were to approach, clumsily, any member of the squad while he was holding his piece bag he would raise a cry of sheer terror: "Watch my flask!" Every time you went to sit down on the hillside or in the back of the lorry, you checked in case one of these precious things was in any danger of tipping over or being broken. This pathological fear for the thermos and its safety was the result of fifties technology. For some bizarre reason, no manufacturer in those days had thought of designing a threaded top that would screw tight and provide a sensible and secure seal so that the top would stay in place should the flask tip over. No, it was a stupid, spongy cork that could easily pop out with the pressure inside the flask or as a result of it receiving even the slightest jolt. This explains the haunted looks and close-encircling arms round the piece bags in the early part of the day.

The Commission also had its own special housing for its workers as well as hostels for unmarried men. Those who lived in these hostels were a very special type. Many were ex-service men who seemed to be quite happy to continue the army-barracks life style you'd imagine they would have been only too keen to get away from. It was a Spartan sort of life and run on recognisably military lines. The similarity lay in the huts, which would not have been out of place in many barracks of the day. Things like the cookhouse helped to keep up the illusion, as did the rows of iron bedsteads in the huts each with its accompanying metal cupboard for personal belongings, and with the iron stove in the centre. These men had their individual eccentricities, as you would expect, but in the main seemed to find the not-too-demanding Forestry life as some kind of refuge. We were excited too at being in the company of men who had actually seen active service in the War and often asked them questions. The Canadian cook was good for this and would tell us all the violent stories that we wanted. He had been a member of a tank crew. There was another, though, who was not so satisfying for our youthful cravings for this kind of excitement. In appearance, he was the archetype of the quiet, inoffensive Forestry worker of those days. Small of features, dressed in faded khaki battledress and wearing a large Cameron Highlander Balmoral at a steep slant. When we first heard that he had been captured at St Valery with the Highland Divisions we thought that we were on to a good thing. But no. It seems that he had spent all of his time as a Prisoner of War working on farms deep in rural Germany that were relatively unscarred by the conflict until the very end of hostilities. While we yearned for details of heel-snapping jack-boots and pale-blue-eyed Nazi brutalities, all we could get from him was that he spent the time doing what he knew best – labouring on farms and being reasonably treated. We were left with the image of him toiling away quietly on Bavarian fields as contentedly as he did in the Highland forests. Not much fun there for us.

The Commission also had its own roads to gain access to its forests.

But the military analogy fails to apply as far as the discipline of the job was concerned. One of the main attractions of working in the Forestry was the lack of discipline in any oppressive form. It was not slackness on the part of the system – more that the workforce had come to an accord with the management over certain contentious areas. "Wet Time" is a good example. This meant that if it was raining you didn't work outdoors. And you didn't have your pay docked. Nor I am I going to say that this arrangement was ever abused too much, but we certainly scanned the skies for any likely-looking, rain-bearing clouds, and collectively willed them to spread over us and do the business. If that happened when we were at the hated weeding in the nurseries, with the endless beds of angry, bristling baby trees, we headed immediately for the sheds at the first spit of rain and out came the packs of cards and the cigarettes.

It was a rather more elaborate ritual when we were out working in the hills. The first thing we did when we came to a suitable spot – when we were on bracken-cutting detail or at "brashing" (pruning the lower branches of standing timber: the word, the onomatopoeic description of dry branches being broken off.) – was to erect the shack. This was just a heavy tarpaulin stretched over a basic wooden frame. This was our shelter if it rained. As the job took us further along the hill, the ganger in charge would get some of the squad to dismantle the shack and reassemble it nearer to hand. It's difficult to convey the sheer satisfaction of the acrid cigarette smoke, the whisper of the cards being dealt and in the background the rattle of rain on the canvas close above our heads. The knowledge that we were still earning our full pay made this so much better than hacking our way down the dim aisles of Sitka Spruce with our pruning saws.

Then there was "Travelling Time". This was the other solace of the Forestry worker. We were always delighted when we were told that we were to be going to some far-flung part of the forest for some task or other. This meant that we would arrive at the Forester's office at the nurseries at Auchterawe at the usual time – that was nine o'clock for the juvenile workforce. Then, at around nine o'clock, we would clamber up into the back of one of the long, thin, Bedford lorries with its grating gears and sudden suspension. There was a canvas-covered frame fixed on to the back and the seating was on low, wooden benches. When we were being taken to the brashing, we would sit in rows on these benches with the long-handled curved saw blades in our hands. We would feel like commandos heading into action. The actual day's work really began when we had reached our starting point on the hillside. Sometimes it could be as much as an hour's journey from base. There was one occasion when we arrived just in time for our morning "blow" (tea-break). That was what we called perfect timing.

At the end of the day it was the same system in reverse. We'd get everything packed up in time to catch the lorry so that it would have us back at the point from where we had left in the morning, at 5pm exactly. Yes, a very civilised arrangement indeed.

The full list of the tasks we were asked to do in the Forestry was as follows: weeding the seedbeds in the huge, immaculate nurseries; cutting bracken growing around the small trees out on the hillsides; pruning the mature standing timber in the various plantations and planting small trees out on the prepared areas of hillside. Sometimes we would be delegated to clear the rides (firebreaks) of any birch trees or other invaders and on one occasion, I accompanied a Forester and a ganger who were calculating the cubic capacity of a hillside above Invermoriston, of its mature standing timber. I walked along with them, clicking a small counter at each tree that was marked. Every tenth one had its girth taken and every hundredth had to be felled to have its measurements taken in all detail. Height as well as girth. It was on such occasions that a little guile on my part could have had some effect on the final accuracy of the calculations. It became clear that the easier the felling of the selected tree was the easier life could be in general. The huge cross-cut saw was the method used then and I was providing half of that effort. So if I saw that the hundredth one was some gnarled monster, I would stay my clicking finger on the counter until a more modest one was marked for felling. Of all the Forestry tasks, I suppose pruning was most popular – mainly because it entailed a lot of travel time – and weeding in the nurseries was the most universally loathed.

In the Fifties, the Forestry Commission planted out the seedlings of the various conifers in huge, open-air nurseries. These were divided up into long beds, about four feet wide and fifty yards or so in length (measurements from memory). There would be several dozens of these beds in each nursery, so we're talking pretty big acreages of land up at Auchterawe to the west of the village of Fort Augustus.

I went back there quite recently, and it was eerie to find that not a trace of them is now left. Nothing remains of the beautifully trimmed hedges that separated the nurseries from each other or of the geometrically exact roadways that provided the access to them.

Back in those days, there was no time to admire such niceties. Close and relentless supervision was the main problem when working at the weeding in the nurseries. When you were working up in the hills there was more sympathy for human weaknesses and our common fallibility. There was the "blow" – the five or ten-minute break for a rest and a smoke. You could set off early back to where the piece bags were left if the pruning or bracken-cutting had taken you far away from base camp. If you had a good ganger in charge you could find all sorts of ways of easing the burden of the daily toil. In the nurseries, there was no chance of this whatsoever. First, and most obvious, you were all day close to – even sometimes in sight of – the Foresters' main office. There was scarce a day when one or other of them would not take a stroll. God help you – or the ganger in charge – if the squad was not back to work within minutes of the end of the tea-break, or if there was any horse-play going on. It's hard to convey the sheer scale of it all. I have already mentioned the large numbers of these long, narrow beds, packed with baby trees. When you had spent most of a morning completing one of these beds, there was no sense of satisfaction because there was always another one lying waiting for you and your aching back. Even the completion of a whole nursery was a muted affair. Just over the hedge lay another vast Matto Grosso of weeds, stretching, it seemed, to the horizon.

The most vital piece of equipment for this hateful job was the weeding stool. Mostly it was just a piece of hessian sacking wrapped into a tight bundle, just thick enough to keep the buttocks away from the dank, chill earth. Some of the old hands made their own, and after quitting the Commission, they might leave them behind. I discovered one such in one of the sheds and claimed it as my own. It was a tiny, truncated thing, with a crude wooden frame and a piece of red carpeting for the seat. I have it fixed in my mind's eye yet.

We worked at the weeding in pairs with your partner sitting on the other side of the bed. From your sitting position you were just able to reach about half way across the bed with comfort. This meant that between the two of you, all the weeds would be taken care of. They were just left scattered in the alley behind you where they were duly raked up and carted away in barrows to be dumped somewhere.

Ideally, you would work with a partner who would move about the same speed. It was not considered the thing to do, to charge on ahead. It wouldn't do you much good anyway.

The tree that was most loathed in the hills was the Sitka Spruce. Its lower branches were dense and impenetrable and its needles were vicious. Added to that, there were the dark mutterings of the old hands of something called "Sitka poisoning" that could strike certain unfortunate people down. Well these vile things were no less obnoxious in their infant state. While weeding them, it was impossible to keep your wrists from being punctured over and over again by their tiny needles. For whole days on end, the insides of the wrists would be ablaze with a rash and a blaze of raw pain. No form of glove or protection could we devise that would stave them off.

But the most abiding bad memory of those days – in the nurseries as well as in the hills – was the hellish persistence of the Highland Midge. Much has been written about this abomination – one of nature's more cynical creations – but nothing can express the abject despair you experience during a still, damp day of weeding while they are at their most lethal. We used everything in the way of accepted wisdom to get even the tiniest scrap of relief. Smoke was considered to be the most effective. Any kind of smoke. Naturally we used this as an excuse to smoke cigarettes. A few adults might have objected to the sight of a squad of schoolchildren lighting up enthusiastically, but with the common enemy drifting around us all in blood-frenzied clouds, no-one really paid all that much heed. Occasionally twists of sacking would be set alight and it smelt so foul that it had to be doing some good. Then there was the final line of defence – the Forestry Commission's very own anti-midge cream. It came in a small, round, shallow tin and it was grey-white and oily. You spread it over all the exposed parts, avoiding the eyes and the mouth. The acrid smell that it gave off had you believe at first that in some laboratory, white-coated scientists had really come up with the answer to our misery. Maybe at last the tiny vile brutes would be deterred. But like all the other palliatives it just didn't do the job in the end. When you were trapped at the weeding, you were at your most helpless and defenceless. Up in the hills, though, you could move about – even flee when things became really bad. Like the occasion when we had set off to another part of the hillside during a spell of bracken-cutting between Fort Augustus and Invermoriston. The ganger was plodding on ahead, and we were strung out in ragged single file behind him. We had our piece bags on our backs and must have looked like some lost platoon in the Burmese jungle. It was still and very humid. Suddenly, we were going down a slope into a fairly small hollow – like a pond of ultra still, moist air – and it was here that the ambush was sprung. From the wet bracken fronds and the tall soaking grass rose unbelievably dense black clouds of midgies. Never had any of us seen them in such vast silent drifts. We soon found that they were getting into our eyes and were clogging up our noses. The frenzied screaming their wings made in our ears added to the sheer terror of the experience. All of us began to run, and soon were breasting the slope at the other side of the depression, and gasping in the tiny breeze we found there that helped to blow away the worst of our tormenters. Yes the midgie held a special place in our nightmares after that.

But to return to the weeding in the nurseries, the only plus factor during these stints was the decent shelter that you had close at hand when the heavens began to tip it down on us. The sheds at the nurseries were large and substantial. They were wind and waterproof and there were piles of materials lying around into which you could settle comfortably at tea breaks or when the rain was hammering down. A genteel faint drizzle wasn't enough to allow you to scuttle for shelter in the closely-supervised regime here. It had to be the real thing. But when that did happen, the two main elements that brought real pleasure were cigarettes and cards. Out would come the greasy packs and pontoon – the only game we played then – ruled the day. Maybe that was because of the Westerns that we watched in the cinema: the eye squinting through the tendril of acrid smoke as you outstared the opposition.

Certainly it is the only tolerable memory of the one Forestry job that has left me a special legacy. I nurture an ever-abiding loathing of gardening to this very day.

Some final memories. One warm afternoon, with a breeze just strong enough to keep the midgies at bay, our squad of about a dozen or so was cutting bracken on a hillside between Invermoriston and Fort Augustus. The bracken was very deep and was completely overwhelming the young trees. We were in one of our silly moods since our ganger was one of the more easy-going ones. In those days we used to compete to see who could have the sharpest "heuk" – the sickle we were given to cut the bracken. We were always borrowing the ganger's sharpening stone to whet the crescent blades to their most purposeful edge. Then we'd try to see who could slice through the thickest branch on a passing birch with one blow. During one of these contests, a blade rebounded and struck the back of my right index-finger. The wound was serious enough for the ganger's first-aid kit to be useless – a fair portion of my finger seemed to be hanging free. I had to head off for my bicycle down beside the main road, far below and head back to Fort Augustus and the doctor. Speedy stitching was required. With my blood-boltered finger held up ahead of me, I started a wild plunge down the hillside through the tall bracken full of yellow-green filtered sunlight, brown drifts of pollen and spores, millions of insects and silence. Then I heard a sound just ahead. It was a heavy droning. I had no time even to try to work out what it might be, when I found myself bursting into a small clearing in the jungle of bracken in which lay the remains of a dead stag. It was partly decomposed and from its corruption exploded an angry shimmering of blue-green flies that blinded and almost choked me. Such an awful image in the middle of the summer softness still has the ability to disturb. And I have still the reminder of that day in the form of a small crinkled crescent of scar on the back of the index finger.

And a final odd recollection. On one part of the hillside up Glenmoriston, we came across tall mounds – about shoulder height made of earth and twigs. The ganger told us that they were ants' nests. We had seen ants many times, but living in huge nests like this? – it was hard to believe. Some of us sliced the tops off one of the nearest of these odd phenomena, and sure enough, the ants were there in their seething masses. I still can see the soldier ants who were defying our brutish intrusion, arching their tiny bodies and lancing their jets of poison or acid at anything held directly above them. In the bright sun, the tiny jets were visible, and I remember the sharp smell of the liquid they sprayed on to my aluminium cigarette case, which I moved just above them. We soon tired of this sport and left them alone.

Mystery in the Elite Squad

During my last spell in the Commission in the late fifties when I was a final year student in Aberdeen University, I got the chance of some piecework.

There were always tales going around of the huge pay packets you could get. These piecework squads were seen as a sort of elite – a commando group who kept their own company and oozed machismo. And so it was that I found myself in the company of three others of similar age and being offered a fortnight's planting trees above Dundreggan in Glenmoriston. Our squad was made up of myself, a long, rangy student from Glasgow called Andy, a student from Oxford – also tall and incredibly fit and whose name I cannot remember – and Stan. Stan was ex-Royal Navy and seemed ill at ease on dry land. He was still in naval garb: pale blue shirt, white singlet and thick white stockings folded down outside his boots. Stan had been on HMS Amethyst (as a cook) and was full of stories of the dash down the Yangtze River during that famous Cold War incident in the late forties.

A new Forester met us at Dundreggan on our first morning. He was young – not much older than ourselves in fact. And he was keen. Very keen. His uniform jacket was brand-new and he had an eager spaniel attached to one of his ankles. No conversation , and he led us silently to the part of the hill we were to be planting on. This was a very important moment: one glance would tell us if we were on to a good thing or not. There was no problem. We were looking at a rolling stretch of hillside that had been newly ploughed. Huge furrows had been gouged out and the dark, peaty soil lay folded back and glistening. This was the very best planting country that you could ask for. The Forester saw to all the final details: the storing in small trenches ("sheuching") of the 100-bundles of tiny trees and the instructions about the exact area to be planted. It would be a simple calculation on the Forester's part to work out how many trees our squad had planted at the end of each day. Nobody was really in charge so all listened carefully. No natural leader had emerged. Stan seemed to be finding it all very alien, though. The Forester and his spaniel then disappeared down the hill.

Well, now it was all up to us. We shouldered our large, floppy canvas bags, filled them up with a suitable number of bundles of trees; each selected a furrow and set off. Cut once, cut twice at right angles, open up the flap of soil, trail the roots in properly, press down the flap and stamp with your heel. It was tiring, repetitious, but it was well within our powers. The rapidly emptying sheuchs of tiny trees told us that all was going to work out just fine for us. Eleven pounds at the end of the week? Maybe fourteen? By the end of that first highly productive day, we had planted about the whole of that ploughed hillside. We were one very contented squad.

The next morning, the Silent Forester was again standing by the gate as we got down from the lorry. He had an unusual looking set of spades propped up against the fence beside him. They had standard handles, but the blades were narrow and pointed. We were to find out why all too soon. And it was decidedly not good news. Instead of another long series of co-operative furrows like the previous day, he led us to a large birch wood that had been "ringed": each tree had a ring cut round the base of the trunk so that it would die fairly soon. Our job was to plant our quota in that doomed birch wood. The spades that had puzzled us were designed to force a space in the tangled fretwork of roots just below the surface. The impassive Forester watched for a spell as we tried to hurl our spades down with enough force to make a hole big enough to insert a plant. Then he strode away on other business. Soon we were all exhausted and dispirited. We cursed the sheer nastiness of the management when we soon realised that there was not the remotest chance of achieving the previous day's results. But we just kept on plunging the bone-jarring spades into the springy mesh of birch roots.

Near the end of that miserable day, the Forester returned. He moved purposefully some fifty yards or so behind where we were still working. Every now and then he would stoop to test how the plants had been put in.

Suddenly, he stood up straight. "Right, you lot! Over here. NOW!"

He was holding out a bunch of plants in his hand – probably about fifty of them. He glared at each of us in turn.

"Which one of you is responsible for this?"

He stepped back a few feet and dragged yet another bedraggled bunch from under the roots of a birch tree. It appeared as if one of our small squad had been cheating on a quite imbecilic scale. Now let me admit here and now, that there were occasions when I'd have no compunction about slipping a few under a flap of moss – more in

frustration at the mean trick that the Commission had played on us –
but huge handfuls like the ones just discovered? Not a chance.

We were yelled at and grilled individually, but no confession
emerged. But the evidence was damning enough, and he threatened
us with instant dismissal unless somebody owned up. "It's down the
bloody hill for the lot of you unless somebody admits to it." came his
chilling ultimatum.

I think it was a combination of the silky persuasiveness of the Oxford
student and the drawling Glasgow confidence of Andy that managed
to calm the storm and had the apoplectic Forester accept that
somebody had just left a few scattered mini-sheuchs and had
forgotten to go back for them. Anyway, he grudgingly accepted this
explanation and headed off, leaving us shaken and even more fed-up.

The true villain never owned up. I know that I didn't do it, so that
leaves three. The lines we had been working on meandered through
the hateful birch wood in such a haphazard way that it was quite
impossible to identify who had been nearest the spot where the rogue
sheuchs had been discovered. No, that wood – even though it was
under sentence of death – kept its secret. But I am fairly certain that it
was Sailor Stan who was the guilty man. Not that it mattered all that
much, because we weren't together for much longer. It was made
clear to us that there were to be no more easy hillsides of ploughing
to be planted, so all that we could be expected to earn was the usual
weekly wage for vastly greater efforts than the rest of the workforce.
It just wasn't worth it so we handed in our pointed spades and
returned, chastened, to the main squad. And that was the
ignominious end to my brief spell as a member of the Forestry
equivalent of the Praetorian Guard.

One other dubious inheritance I have gained from those far-off days
in the Forestry Commission is a chilling reminder of the swift
passage of time. The sight of that particular wooded stretch of
former moorland, immediately to the west of Dundreggan Dam in
Glenmoriston, always brings a moment of inner stillness. In the mid-
fifties, along with a number of my carefree contemporaries, I planted
my share of these larch and spruce trees. Then, they were tiny, limp
bedraggled wisps of life and we were rather less than tender as we
jabbed them into the earth. Now, I drive past a plantation of tall,
aloof and disturbingly mature-looking trees and try to tell myself that
it isn't all that significant. After all, they were chosen by the

Commission in those days for their high timber yield and speedy growth. But that really is of no help. On one of those occasions when I was heading west, my old Forestry instincts stirred. I found myself thinking that they could do with a spot of brashing.

And a very last Forestry memory. One day as we arrived back down at the roadside after a day high in the hills, we were in lively Friday evening high spirits. It was payday. We saw a large chromium-glittering tourist bus surging along the road towards us. On some impulse or other, we decided to act out the part of primitive native tribes people who were encountering civilisation for the very first time. We stood in a row, staring in mock amazement at the approaching bus with its rows of elderly heads turned towards us. Then we pretended huge alarm, then terror. We hurled away our bags and tools and ran frantically back from the road and dived behind a bank of heather. We then timidly raised our heads and peered at the now-bemused tourists, some of whom were by now pointing cameras at us. What tales they brought back to Essex or Surbiton of the primitive Highlands we'll never know, but I am sure we didn't do our reputation much good with that rather daft exhibition.

In the Dry Canteen

As you drive along the tree-lined road towards Invergarry by Loch Oich side, you might notice on your right, a low, stone building. It has the look of something constructed by craftsmen, is blended into the immediate surroundings and is totally unobtrusive. No hint is there of the huge excavations that accompanied its construction in the late fifties during the Hydro-Electric revolution in the Highlands. This is one of the many power stations into which the waters of Highland lochs and rivers were channelled for the generating of hydro electricity. The memories of these times – almost a life-time ago - are still pretty close to the surface even now because of the immense impact these events had upon those of us who lived through them. They were indeed frenetic times, when a new breed of man moved among us – the "tunnel tiger". They were the days when we felt that our part of Scotland was actually being noticed and being helped into the twentieth century by a caring administration. History had told us that up till then all we normally had to expect was to be patronised, exploited or just plain ignored. It really is extraordinary to look back on the days of the Hydro Schemes in the nineteen fifties – distance in time merely lends to the sheer unlikeliness of it all. They were the Klondike days in our village and in the neighbouring communities; they were the frontier times. Huge ex-army vehicles churned on their way in convoys: workers' buses – bare and wooden-seated – lined up to take the men of the village to their jobs in the tunnels and at the dams every morning and brought them back again at night. Near my own village of Fort Augustus there were several of these vast engineering projects – though none actually at it. There were Dundreggan Dam, Cluanie Dam – both up Glenmoriston – and Mullardoch Dam – each of these with attendant tunnels and power stations. Further away was the Glen Quoich project where my cousin Joan worked as a secretary – drawn there by a romantic notion of the Highlands from her job at the very centre of government in Westminster. The vast energy of these undertakings – the sheer scale of what was being done by men and machines in the hills and glens – communicated itself to all of us in the village. We were always aware of what was going on and often discussed the latest milestones or even tragedies. There would be tension, for example, when a tunnel was about to break through. One of them, I recollect, had the two teams of tunnelers set out from opposite sides of a hill range, aiming to meet deep in the middle of the immense rock mass. To anyone ignorant of the skills of the engineers it seemed an impossible task. The tunnels met exactly, of course, and celebrations ensued.

The engineers who came with the schemes enjoyed a kind of respect in our village that the profession claims it never gets in society today. They were our fifties equivalent of a sort of jet set. They lived in smartly designed houses or restored older properties. They were mainly young and personable. They drove around in the then equivalent of the Range Rover of today: the rugged Land Rover (then quite a recent innovation). They dressed in the equivalent of today's Barbour Jacket and green boots – the heavy, camel-hair duffel coat – and so on it went. We were quite envious of them with their relaxed bearing and air of easy confidence. They also took leading parts in the running of many of the village activities.

When the dams were being built, cranes bristled around them and the noise of the monsters that moved the earth and boulders was overpowering. There was always a sense of urgency. It was a strange experience to look up the length of a glen behind one of these slowly rising grey walls of concrete and try to imagine what it would look like when the vegetation, roads and occasional small houses were submerged below an immense sheet of grey water. Yet when you pass by these places today almost fifty years later, they look as old as the hills themselves and the lochs that formed behind them seem just as timeless.

The great Power Stations that hold the generators were built mainly of finest building stone – local stone as well – and were meant to blend in as much as possible with their surroundings. They were designed to complement their environment, not to clash or jar the senses. Landscaping was lavish and on the whole this was carried out with scrupulous care. The knowledge that glens might be drowned and the configuration of the landscape changed for ever seemed to drive the planners to make a corresponding effort to offend as little as possible. I would suggest that in this they have had a measure of success. Though it prompts one to wonder what might have been the story if these had been planned and built by the generation who despoiled the following decade – one made infamous with the sheer brutality of its design and architecture.

From the outset, there were opportunities for casual student jobs on these schemes, from labouring on the surface or underground, to maybe being chain-man for an engineer. The man to approach for one of these jobs was known by the odd title of "Steam Boss". The Steam Boss for the Invergarry scheme had his office in a small, dark-green, portable cabin that stood right by the roadside at the place where the vast holes were being gouged out of the rock for the power station that was to be installed there. The day I called, this enormously wide and deep shaft was well on its way to completion. I asked the man behind the desk (Jimmy Anderson, as I recall) what chance there was for something available by way of labouring. I had the exciting notion that I might even be able to join the already legendary "tunnel tigers" who were the shock troops of all these schemes. I might even get to wear some kind of helmet and earn very large amounts of money. But no, it was not to be. Instead, I was told that the camp shop (or "Dry Canteen" – explanation later) required an assistant immediately. That would have to do. The huge camp for the work force was several miles further up the road, just beyond the village of Invergarry on a level field near the river. Needless to say, not the tiniest trace of it remains today nearly half a century later. I had the greatest difficulty pinpointing where it had been when I made a recent visit - not helped by the fact that the old road has long vanished and been replaced by the modern wide sweep of the new road to the Isles. But in the early fifties, it was the location of a large, exclusively masculine community that had its own crude, basic dynamic. The huts stood in rows and were bleakly functional – the kind associated with prisoner of war camps or army barracks. Each of the men who lived in them had his own iron bedstead and simple locker for possessions. This absolute bareness and minimal comfort provision didn't seem to bother the men all that much.   They expected nothing more from the raw life-style of their calling.

And raw it was indeed. The men who worked in the tunnels (the "Tunnel Tigers" of legend) were the ones at the sharp end. Their job was as grinding as it was desperately dangerous. Explosions tore at the rock deep inside the hills, and these men had to live with the swirling dust, stunning noise and the dull artificial light for the greater part of every working day. Safety regulations in the fifties were primitive as was the equipment for pumping out the foul air – after every shot at the face, the "jelly reek" (acrid fumes from the gelignite explosives) would hang heavy and find its way deep into the lungs of all in its vicinity. On one of the few occasions that I actually entered this world, I was reminded just how dangerous it was. I had every afternoon off when working in the Dry Canteen. With the camp all but empty during the day, my hours of business were from early morning to forenoon and from early evening to around ten o'clock at night. The rest of the long day was all my own to pass the time as I wished. I would sometimes head off to the site of the power station or cycle up to the immense workings at the dam at Dundreggan and just watch. I got to know many of the workmen, and one who controlled a huge crane that lowered equipment into the abyss of the excavation for the power station would let me join him in the cabin. I remember the nausea of the sufferer from vertigo when I would look down into the giddy depths below my feet. On another occasion, one of the foremen took me down to the bottom of that pit in the rock, and then led me along a tunnel that joined up with it – presumably the one that would convey the pent-up mass of the water from the distant dam into the generators. The concrete sleeve for lining this tunnel had not yet been fitted properly in place, so that I had to squeeze between the outside of this sleeve and the actual bare rock of the tunnel. Just ahead of us was the surge shaft that went right up to the surface, far above us. Some light filtered down from the far-away world above and water dripped incessantly. My guide let me look briefly up to the distant, tiny circle of sky, and I remember vertigo getting me here – even in reverse. As we turned to head back to the power station chamber, there came a hollow booming and crashing from the shaft just behind us and then we saw a series of large baulks of timber leaping and splintering on the rocky floor with the force of their impact. It was all too clear what might have happened to me and my guide had we been just a matter of seconds later – just as it was clear to me that a job in the Dry Canteen was in many ways preferable to the dubious thrills of the life of a tunnel tiger.

And so, it was to the Invergarry Camp and the Dry Canteen that I set out each morning in the workmen's bus from Fort Augustus, heaving my bike in through the back door and propping it up in the aisle between the wooden-slatted seats. These were still the days when simple creature comforts for workers such as upholstery in bus seats were not deemed appropriate. I had to cycle the nine or ten miles back home every night because I finished too late to catch a service bus or get a lift from a works vehicle. And that odd name for my workplace: just to distinguish it from the "Wet" Canteen, which was the beer (only) bar. The Dry Canteen was indeed a very odd place – just what really you might expect to find in frontier country: a kind of typical frontier general store in fact. There was a manager there already – a silent, remote man who took minimum interest in me and troubled me even less. Just enough to show me the basic things that had to be done and then he let me get on with it. If I kept the floors swept and served the queues of workmen at the large counter with minimum fuss and without bothering him, then all was well as far as he was concerned. An excellent arrangement. I sold cigarettes in vast quantities; biscuits, hot mugs of tea from an enormous urn, everything down to the last detail of haberdashery, snacks, newly-baked pancakes that were delivered from the adjoining cookhouse (buttered by me as well) – in fact everything you could imagine from a general store. There was also a substantial section that sold clothes and footgear – boots, shoes in sort of basic styles. This was the age of the Teddy Boy and the shirts, jackets, ties and accessories reflected it. I stood myself a pair of shoes on one occasion. They were what we called "brothel creepers" in those days: ox-blood red and with thick, squashy, crêpe soles. I can see them clearly yet. I had two meals in the cookhouse each day – one at midday and the other in the evening. There was a door behind the counter that opened into a narrow passage that led right into the kitchens. This was where the gigantic vats of stew and cauldrons of boiled potatoes simmered and where all the rest of the basic uncompromising fare was prepared. All of this was presided over by one of the most villainous, blue-jowled, sinister-looking men I have ever met in the flesh. He was a clone of that evil-looking Western Hollywood actor, Lee Van Cleef. But he was as pleasant and generous a man as you could ever want to meet in such a job and he always saw to me getting extra helpings whenever I wanted them. His name was Mick and what else could he be but Irish.

The overwhelming presence of Irish in the workforce that lived in the Invergarry workers' camp was soon obvious – just as were the clichés of working hard and playing harder. Every Friday, the timekeepers would set up their trestle tables in the Dry Canteen, just inside the door, and the workers would file past them to pick up their pay packets. These were briefly scrutinised and then ripped open with the envelopes just dropping on the floor. A swift stride to the counter then for huge orders of cigarettes. A hard weekend of booze would follow for many of these men and visits to local dance-halls were obvious outlets for them too. They were often kind and spontaneous as well. On the fairly regular occasions when there might have been an accident in a tunnel or elsewhere on the worksite and where serious injuries might have resulted (or even a fatality) I would be asked to set out a collection box on the counter. On payday, notes would be crammed in and this money would then be sent back to an address in Ireland – to the parents or wife of the unfortunate victim. It was always a shock to me to see the enormous pays that these men earned. I used to look at the discarded pay packets when I was sweeping up the floor at the end of the day. I knew enough about the nature of the job they were doing not to begrudge them a single penny of it though.

There was one feature that made the long afternoons more than tolerable: the magnificent, full-size snooker table that had been installed in an adjoining room. It was in immaculate condition and everything was in place from the sets of gleaming coloured snooker balls, to the row of smart cues in their rack and the score board on the wall. I have mentioned that my hours were from nine in the morning till about one o'clock. The canteen was then shut till around five o'clock in the evening. (I really cannot recollect the exact times from this distance). The afternoons would have been pretty intolerable if I could only go around exploring the surrounding country on my bike. The barman from the Wet Canteen and I got on pretty well. He was in his twenties and wise in the ways of the world and that included a fair degree of skill on the snooker table. I had had my first year at Aberdeen University and had already been drawn into the seductive world of the snooker hall at the students' union. Now I was able to misspend my youth to my heart's content without it costing me a penny. And I was able to put in such a power of practice that it would be sure to stand me in good stead when I began the new term.

The massive support legs of the snooker table were to save me during one seriously weird episode though. A little background first. There was a stocky local youth who did odd-jobs around the camp during the day. All I remember was that his name was Jackie. He would shift coal and other heavy loads around in barrows or hand carts and was a simple sort of fellow. Just part of the daily background and as unthreatening as the average passing butterfly. He would drop into the Dry Canteen regularly around the same time each day when it was closed – tapping on the door to let me know he was there. His favourite was a glass of milk that I poured for him. There would be a scrap of cheery chat and that was about it. On one of these occasions, things developed in a rather startlingly different manner. There was the usual tap on the door, and I poured the glass of milk for him. I have no idea if there was the usual bit of banter, but I suddenly found myself drenched in milk as Jackie threw the contents of the glass right in my face. Before I could even wipe it from my eyes, I was hurled to the floor by the weight of the odd-job man who had rushed behind the counter and attacked me. There then followed such a bizarre grunting and heaving, and idiotic wrestling – all the time with me trying to find if this was a real attack of just some sort of mad prank on his part. It soon became clear that is was no joke. Jackie was out to do me pretty serious injury. As we were by now scuffling on the floor out beyond the counter, I really began to panic. I was alone in the building. The silent manager was away and the cookhouse was well beyond earshot. It was all between me and the odd-job man – and he was a damned sight stronger than I. It was now that the snooker table took centre stage and came to the rescue. We had lurched, heaving and grunting, into the billiard room, still locked in lunatic embrace, when slowly we toppled to the floor. A dull, soft thud immediately below me said that something had made contact with my attacker. It was the thump of his head hitting one of the table legs. And that was the end of the crisis. After a few moments, he was blinking back to consciousness. He looked at me, grinning and rubbing the back of his head. Absolutely nothing about what just happened. I watched him walking out of the canteen, muttering vaguely to himself and wondered what the outcome would have been if that billiard table leg had not made such welcome contact. The next day, Jackie the odd-job man was back in the Dry Canteen for his glass of milk and banter and for the rest of my time working there that summer, there was no further reference to his ferocious brain-storm. Mind you, every time he came in when I was alone, I made sure that the counter flap was down and fixed in place. Just in case.

However strange this episode might seem, the fact is that I didn't do anything about it at the time. I could have reported him to the camp manager, but chose not to. This man was a silent, humourless specimen, heavily-built, pasty-white and ponderous of movement. He was a man I really had no wish have to approach about anything. I always had the feeling that in the frontier atmosphere of that workmen's camp, a student employee was especially vulnerable. Dismissal could be peremptory and at the whim of a boss. And there was no court of appeal.

My one real abiding memory of that summer holiday job is the sight of the gaunt, grey faces of the tunnel workers after they had shuffled past the timekeepers' trestle table and picked up and signed for their pay packets. The ritual was always the same. The envelope was ripped open and the folded notes were riffled through, then there was a swift stride towards my counter. "A hondred (sic) Capstan, Full Strength." Was a fairly standard order and sometimes followed by, "See you at the dance, son. Maybe it's me lucky night tonight."

They were a breed of men who burned themselves out quickly. Generous pay that came in bursts could be spent as suddenly. Many saved by sending cash back to their relatives in Ireland, but many also lived by excess of hard work and excess of – just excess. Without them and their ferocious energy and carelessness about personal safety and well-being, these vast Hydro Electric dams and power stations that lie so serenely as a natural part of our scenery today would never have come into existence.

Placating the Captain
("Do you say 'Sir' to your father?")

When I set out to apply for a job as a ghillie on the Glenmoriston Estates, it was in the opposite direction I had to go – west to Invergarry. The proprietor of the Invergarry Hotel, Captain Hunt, had the licence then to shoot on these hills.

On that day, my main concern was to make as good an impression on the Captain as I could. He had a reputation for holding a low opinion of the proletariat in general, and of the native Highlander in particular. One clue pointing to this was the provision he made for the local pub clientele. His public bar was about the dingiest and most uncomfortable of its kind in the whole Great Glen. So I got myself up in my standard nineteen fifties student walking-out uniform. This consisted of navy blazer with silver buttons and sunburst Aberdeen University badge on the breast pocket; white shirt with badge-bespangled tie – and over it all was draped the raffishly casual, open-hanging duffel coat. My impeccable middle class credentials were all there on display.

It was a truly amazing experience. Captain Hunt was far and away the most condescendingly, patrician presence in which I have ever found myself. Yet in an odd way, it is only heavy-duty tweed and a voice that had the very essence of the accents of the ascendancy that I am able to recall. I have no image of his features whatsoever in my memory. My attempts to answer his bizarre questions came in fits and starts and it rapidly dawned on me that I wasn't making a very good impression. I really wanted this job and it seemed to be slipping away. I was desperate to get it.

The inquisition stopped abruptly. He stared at me directly through his monocle (I don't know if he actually had one; but he should have).

"Tell me," he barked. "Do you say 'Sir' to your father?"

The total absurdity of it.

I have no idea as to how I responded to this, but the outcome of it all was that I found myself at the receiving end of a lofty sermon on to how I was to comport myself while in his employment. I was at all times to address him (Captain Hunt) as "Sir". Similarly, all male guests that I would accompany into the hills. Women were to be called "Madam" or "Miss" where appropriate. I was NEVER to address any of them unless I was first spoken to and I was NEVER,

EVER to walk ahead of them. A sharp lesson on the realities of the class system to shake my timid early leanings towards liberalism.

If this was fiction, I suppose I would have reared up with fierce Highland pride and flashed my eyes in defiance at such humiliating conditions. The Captain would have found himself skewered to his front door by a dagger of Oscar Wildean wit as I stalked proudly on my way.

That wasn't what happened, of course, and I was just glad that, somehow, I had persuaded him I could do the job. Actually, it wasn't a full ghillie's job I was taken on for, but initially a gun-bearer and later a pony man.

Sometimes, the guests would travel in their own cars from the Invergarry Hotel to the Glenmoriston Estate. This took them through Fort Augustus, down Loch Ness side to Invermoriston, then up the Glen a further five or six miles to the Lodge which was our base and where the stables and various outhouses were. On such occasions, I would be picked up at Fort Augustus. And now came the next cultural shock after the encounter with the Captain. On the first day, I waited at the roadside in my standard outdoor gear of those days. It was the same as my forestry rig-out – ex-army battledress khaki with heavy blunt-toed tackety boots and gaiters. My piece, flask and additional waterproofs were in my army haversack. A white Jaguar oozed up alongside me and stopped. There were two people in the car: the driver was an elderly, military-looking type with aggressive snout on his bonnet and with a bristling moustache. His companion was much younger, and also looked officer material. As I reached out for the rear door-handle, the driver swiftly emerged.

"One moment, ghillie," he snapped. He went to the back of the car and opened the boot. He removed some sheets of paper then reached in and spread them over the dimpled leather of the rear seat.

"You can get in now, ghillie."

And these were the last words addressed to me for the rest of that journey. It was the bizarre conversation between the two of them – sometimes about rather personal matters – that made me realise that I was in the presence of aliens. They quite simply did not see me. I did not register on their senses. They spoke to each other as they would in the presence of their servants, which is what I now was. It didn't matter if I heard what they were saying any more than if I had been just an item of hunting equipment lying on the back seat.

I met many more of these strange people over the several weeks I spent at that job, and in the main, they tended to behave in the same way towards me. They were mostly, but not exclusively, English and the obvious thing they shared was that they were all seriously rich. But whatever airs these guests might have given themselves, in the presence of the gamekeeper, they had to show a certain deference. I have no memory of the name of the one who ruled the Glenmoriston Estates when I was there, but he was an archetype of the species in all details. Plus-four suit of armoured tweed; fore-and-aft; enormous brogues with flapping leather tongues; reddened, wind-scoured face and pale, rain-washed eyes. He was silent as the hills and seemed to re-direct the normal human instinct for his own kind into a total absorption in the wilds. He had not the slightest of sentimental feelings for the animals he guarded and culled but had a deep respect that came from his vast, accumulated knowledge of them. This meant that he had a pretty low estimation of those who lived communally in towns and cities – or even villages. As for me, I don't think he actually disliked me personally. It's just that I was a dilettante student who was idling away a few holiday weeks, toying with elements of what was to him a life's commitment. There were to be occasions when I would wince under his undisguised contempt, though.

My first, and most unpleasant, duties were gun-bearing. That's all it was. I had to carry the guest's rifle and follow close behind the deer-stalking party during the long tedious slog to get there and then right into the theatre of the actual event itself. During the final stages, I had to crawl through the heather with the rifle carried in the crook of my elbows. One particular episode stands out which illustrates the more unpleasant aspects of deer-stalking – certainly from the lowly viewpoint of the gun-bearer. There were three of us in the party.

The gamekeeper, the guest and myself. We had been moving cautiously for several miles along exhausting hillsides, down into gullies and back up again. The guest on this occasion was middle aged and looked quite absurd in the khaki shorts he had chosen to wear. More than useless protection from the tick-infested heather that we would be crawling through. Suddenly we were all lying flat and absolutely still. The gamekeeper and guest were a few yards ahead of me, with the gamekeeper, naturally, in front. Now we were all crawling very slowly up the last few feet of a slope to the crest of a small hill. A signal from the gamekeeper told me to lie absolutely still. He had taken his telescope out of its case and extended it silently. For a minute or two he stared intently through it. Then he gestured to me to pass forward the expensive rifle I had been carrying up till now. Now he loaded it carefully, easing the cartridges silently into the magazine. He glanced again over the tussock he was using for cover and adjusted the sights. It was only then that the carefully prepared weapon was passed to the guest after which he helped him into a more comfortable shooting position. Now he set the sights of his own rifle, drew back the bolt and slid it soundlessly into the firing position. He gave another tiny gesture and now all the guest had to do (and what he had paid a very large amount of money to do) was to squeeze the trigger and kill the stag or hind that the skills of the gamekeeper had set up for him.

The sound of the shot rolled over the depression, still out of sight to me where I was crouching, to be followed almost immediately by another from the gamekeeper's rifle. Either the guest has missed the animal completely or had only wounded it so that the gamekeeper had to finish the job. There were no more shots. It wasn't long till we came to the russet and dun-coloured corpse with its staring eye and protruding tongue. There was a heavy gash on its neck and further down, the dark blossom where the gamekeeper's bullet had felled it.

I knew enough about the next stage of the proceedings to find something to do while the gruesome business of the gralloching was taking place. I probably lit a small, smoky fire to guide the pony man to the spot so that he could take the stag back down the hill to one of the outhouses at the Lodge where it would be hoisted up and hung on a hook. As for the guest, the antlered head was his trophy and it would end up being mounted as a testament to his hunting skills.

This rather unpleasant side of the deer-stalking job soon came to an end, and I was told that from now on, I was to be a pony man. This was indeed promotion, but it too had its downside. The first and most obvious was that I knew absolutely nothing about horses. I considered myself a country lad, but had never stood close enough to a horse actually to touch one. And I had never really felt the urge. Yet, here I was, expected to lead an enormous, black beast many miles into the hills and spend up to twelve consecutive hours in its looming, threatening company.

It was while demonstrating how I was to put the weirdly complex saddle on the animal's back that the gamekeeper let slip the mask and make obvious what he really thought of me. And it wasn't very flattering either. As he fired the curt instructions he adopted a sort of slight cocking of the head and a tiny raising of the eyebrow. But it was his querulous, quirky smile that had me sense he considered me a sort of harmless idiot. And that saddle that I have called weirdly complex. It was like no saddle I had ever seen up till then – though remembering that these had been exclusively confined to the cinema screen. It was designed to carry the dead animal off the hill and was never intended to be sat upon. I had seen one of my predecessor ponymen doing just that, but nothing would have tempted me to try it. Not even if it meant being carried over the worst of the grinding slopes of the outward journey. The saddle was black and had a confusion of straps and buckles attached to it – and it was very, very heavy. It had to be thoroughly cleaned after it had been smeared with the gore of a dead stag. To place it on the horse's back was a fearsome task for me. I would heave and grunt to lift it into place while the huge beast sidled and shifted in infuriatingly casual non-co-operation. When it had been settled into place, next came the tightening of the girth strap to ensure that the whole contraption didn't slide slowly upside down under the horse's belly. That did happen on one occasion when I was far into the hills. I had been heading off to reach the place where the kill had taken place and became aware that the saddle had slipped right round. There followed a nightmare of sweating and cursing and hauling to get it back into place, and all the while I was aware that about a couple of miles away, a pale eye was fixed to a telescope and watching my feeble efforts as the afternoon was slipping remorselessly away. The gamekeeper would have a few well-chosen savage comments to shred the last of my self-confidence when I eventually made it to the rendezvous.

The pony man's job was pretty basic – in theory, that is. First you would accompany the shooting party for a fair distance into the hills, plodding along at the rear. Remember – never speak unless you have been spoken to. The gamekeeper had already worked out in advance where the day's kill was most likely to be found and I would be told where I would have to wait for the signal. I would be directed to the top of a hill that commanded a suitable sweep of the surrounding country and would allow me to pin-point the spot where the pick-up was to take place.

During the period I spent in the Glenmoriston hills that year, the weather happened to be, on the whole, very good. I really enjoyed the feeling of absolute insignificance that the hugeness of the landscape forced on you. I was fully equipped in case of downpours with an old army gas-cape to huddle under; it was totally waterproof. And I had a pack of Senior Service, my flask and packet of sandwiches and a book to read. On the frequent calm days, the only sound might be the snuffling and tearing as the horse's yellow teeth snatched at whatever it could find to eat in the heather, and the jingling of its harness. That and its chronic, appalling flatulence.

As the day wore on, a point would come round about early to mid-afternoon when I would allow myself to dare to think that there might not be a kill that day. I would know this if I saw the party appear in the distance on the track that led back down into the glen. I would gather up my belongings and head off down with the horse to tag on behind them. I would be really elated at the prospect of getting home early for a change. But this outcome was quite rare for the obvious reason that the guests would be less than thrilled at spending a fruitless day in the hills. They had paid large sums of money and they wanted to kill deer. All the skills of the gamekeeper would be brought to the fore to make certain that this craving was catered for. The usual outcome of a day's vigilance on my part would be hearing the distant sound of a shot or shots rolling over the hills towards me. This would be followed soon after by either a shrill whistle if the kill had taken place not too far away, but usually it was a plume of smoke from a small heather fire that would be my guide.

One of those seemingly routine days lives forever in my nightmares. The weather had been close and there was only the slightest breeze. I had just got beyond the "please God let me get home early" point when the cursed rifle spoke from somewhere beyond the huge bowl of the hills I had spent the day looking over. I spat out the standard monosyllabic curse and lifted the stone from the rope that tethered the horse. It was particularly galling in that it was Friday and plans had been tentatively made for the evening. There was a dance in the local hall and I was going to meet some of the lads in Inchnacardoch Hotel for a few drinks before the main feature. Pubs in those days closed at nine o'clock, but blessed Inchnacardoch allowed some humanity to temper the Calvinistic licensing laws of those days – mainly because it was a few miles away from the village. Rapid calculation told me that it would take about an hour to get to the pick-up point, twenty minutes to get the beast loaded on to the horse and secured; the long slog back to the Lodge – about four miles at least – followed by a frenzy of cleaning-up, stabling the horse, cleaning the saddle and the other equipment: all that before I could even think about getting back to Fort Augustus. I'd be lucky to get back by eight at the earliest. Hell and damnation.

So I set off down the gentle slope into the depression, through the heather and scattered boulders. As I went down further, my immediate surroundings became greener and more inviting. Still no trees though. On and on we went, with the heavy thudding and jingling of the big black horse close behind me. I had noticed that the air was getting more still and close. The light breezes of higher up were not making it to down here – a part of the hillscape I had not visited before. I noticed now that it was becoming quite warm now – oppressive even. Tall bracken had to be swept aside and this was releasing drifts of midgies, flies and clegs that were beginning to make life more and more unpleasant. Somewhere ahead was a burn that meandered its way across the bowl of the depression before spilling over the edge and tumbling into the glen below. I could just hear it now.

Deep in the stillness of the bracken's hazy fronds and it was now that the horse stopped dead in its tracks.

I was jerked to a halt too, and looked round to see what was happening. The big horse had its head raised slightly and it was snuffling and breathing heavily. I gave a nervous tug on the rope attached to the bridle. Nothing. I tugged again with a bit more force but all that this did was to make the head sway more alarmingly. Its yellow eyes, I noticed, were now rolling in their sockets and everything seemed to be telling me that the creature was in the grip of some dread of imminent danger. But what in God's name could it be? For the next few desperate minutes I tried everything in my pathetically limited experience to get the accursed animal to move forward - all the time aware of the certainty that about a mile or so to the north, that pale eye was fixed to the telescope, taking in the farcical unfolding of events. The gamekeeper would be desperate for the day to end with the minimum of fuss and for the guests to be in the mood to hand out generous tips. As already mentioned, the gamekeeper had a pretty low opinion of me. Usually, though, up till now, I had managed to acquit myself well enough in all the job demanded of me. Now I found myself stuck in the centre of this vast green bowl in the hills. I was trapped among the towering bracken stems in the stifling heat and being choked by the clouds of maddening insects. I was drenched in sweat and embarrassment – but mainly I was in dread of what the gamekeeper would say to me when I would eventually make it to the pick up point. More useless heaving on the rope. I shouted and cursed and wrenched. I'm not sure I didn't lash the huge twitching flanks of that accursed beast, but there was nothing I could do that would make it move one centimetre further forward. Frustration had me almost weeping at the prospect of the gamekeeper, his patience run out, bursting through the bracken to take charge of the horse himself. It was then that I noticed that if I tugged a bit to the left instead of directly forward, the horse would sidle in that direction. I continued with this and found that it would move in a shallow angle – round the centre of the depression instead of directly crossing it as I had intended. It would take about twice the time it should to get there, but that didn't matter. Progress was now being made.

Eventually, I breasted the final slope and reached the spot where wisps of smoke from the signal fire were still drifting in the light breeze. The gamekeeper was glaring at me. The two guests, a pair of languid young men, were lying out flat in the heather. Hip flasks for whisky were in evidence and the gralloched stag was lying limp close by.

"That horse has more bloody sense than you, sonny,"

"It wouldn't do a thing for me. I couldn't help it. How do you mean, 'more sense'?"

"Haven't you worked it out yet – sonny?" (He liked that way of addressing me.)

The now-familiar, talking-to-an-imbecile expression was in place.

"If you'd gone on straight, you would have wound up in the middle of a bog. Didn't you feel the ground getting softer as you got closer to the burn?"

He pointed down to the centre of the vast depression. "The horse would have sunk to its belly in it. Just as bloody well for you it stopped."

He glanced back at the two guests who were smiling in vague amusement at this contretemps among the servants.

And yes – I was utterly crushed. I loathed the gamekeeper at that moment. It was all the worse for me in that I had worked at various quite demanding jobs in the hills over the years and thought that I knew my way around pretty well. I was no ignorant townie let loose on the slopes. So my pride was well and truly mauled.

But there was to be an amazing upturn in events just around the corner: revenge was very close at hand. Its sweetness lay in the fact that it was totally and utterly unexpected. And I did not have to raise a finger myself.

We struggled to get the stag, a pretty heavy one, hauled up on to the saddle and securely strapped down. The antlered head was bent back so that the points might not stab the horse's flanks. Then we set off slowly towards the path back to the Lodge.

"I'll take the horse. You can carry the guns," the gamekeeper said to me. It was my final dismissal and humiliation. The only good thing about it all was that I only had a couple of days left in the job and I would then be shot of this grimly unpleasant man for good. We headed back by a different path to the one I had arrived by. I watched the horse ahead of me as it strained with the weight of the stag on its back. It was thudding along in its methodical, patient way when it began to slow. The gamekeeper gave a sharp tug on the bridle and it speeded up a little, but it seemed to me that it was holding back. Having been here, as it were, a short time ago, I sensed something familiar. But a few barking commands from the gamekeeper and further tugging and the former pace was resumed. The ground was firm though fairly wet.

Violent events now followed swiftly upon each other. The hind legs of the horse began to push violently against the ground which had suddenly and treacherously begun to give way. In as few moments it takes to tell, the whole of the now-terrified animal's hindquarters were being sucked into the trap that had been lying in wait for it. It was now jammed tight in the wet, clinging peat. It was frightful to witness its reactions. It tried to rear up as it surged hopelessly to try to break free. But the enormous dead weight of the stag on its back was forcing it further and further in. The final horror for us all who were there was the appalling strangled sound that the horse was making in its deadly panic. The gamekeeper was well and truly panicking as well at this point. He bellowed hoarsely at us all to help. We tore at the buckles holding down the stag and soon it was toppled from the saddle. It was only then that the trapped animal was able to break free and lash out its rear hooves in triumph. He led it on to drier ground and let it calm down gradually. Then all of us heaved the stag back up on to its back and we set off down the hill once more.

Not too much conversation at this point. Hanging in the air was the spectacular loss of face the gamekeeper had just suffered. He had forgotten it seemed that the additional weight of the stag on the horse's back would have it sink in places it could normally pass safely over. For one of his experience, it was quite astonishing. I could not make up my mind if he was enraged that it had all happened in front of me or the guests. It was usual for them to hand out tips after a successful stalk. Maybe they might not be so generous today.

As far as these tips were concerned, I didn't get much benefit from them. Sometimes a ten-shilling note might find its way into my pocket from a member of a party. Sometimes even, if the gamekeeper had got an especially large one and was feeling more sort of human towards me, he might spin a half crown in my direction. This was rare though. There was one occasion when I did manage to score rather spectacularly in the tipping stakes. It was my last day as ponyman and the stalk had been successful. Things were being sorted out at the outhouses and stable when one of the guests that day suddenly appeared at the door of the stable. With only the barest of communication, he handed me a small sheaf of notes. They were single pound notes, and memory tells me that there were five of them. My pay at this job was around ten pounds per week, so this was an amazing addition to it. My senses were still reeling, and I was heading towards my lift back to Fort Augustus, when I encountered the gamekeeper. There were no farewell speeches from either of us: it was not that kind of relationship as has been made very clear by now. However, he did say, with more than a touch of venom in his tones: "I get them one of the finest beasts on the hill, and not a damn thing for a tip." And the familiar scowl was directed at me.

What should I do? It was obvious that somehow the tip meant for him had come to me. But why on earth had it happened? Either the guest had totally lost the plot, or he had imagined that I would pass it on to its proper recipient. Well, the guest was already heading swiftly down the glen in his transport and was well beyond giving the game away. He had presented me such a marvellous chance to get one over this humourless man. I took it. I headed to the Land Rover and said nothing. There was no chance that our paths would ever cross again. It was a small triumph but an immensely satisfying one. And it tasted so very sweet.

Village Dances

Like most village dances in the fifties, the ones in Fort Augustus and the neighbouring villages were the usual mixture of prim good manners and crude animal excess. Ours were held regularly in the village hall, quite near the schoolhouse, up at the top of Bunoich Brae. Just across the narrow road and behind its protecting wall, the Free Church manse glowered.

On your own patch in your home village you were normally a bit constrained in your behaviour for the obvious reason that there were too many people there who knew you. However, if you were to head off west to Invergarry or east to Invermoriston in the hired bus from Grant's garage, a degree of madness could enter the soul. A glance at the activities of invading armies down through the ages is all that is needed to illustrate this.

The young Highland male of those days was warped by genes and environment to be totally incapable of meeting girls and shuffling round a dance floor with arms around them without the treacherous assistance of alcohol. Just how repellent we made ourselves to the objects of our desires never really seemed to get through to us. When we were sober, a fifties dance floor, with rows of girls in the flouncy dresses of the era, was a place of dread. Yes, a few of our number did have the suave confidence to move easily across the floor to ask the best looking up for a dance – God, how I loathed them and their oily charms. I was one of the majority outside the hall, hunched round the half-bottles of whisky until the essential drink-fuelled level of confidence had been reached. And while on the matter of whisky, it always amazed me in those days how anyone could ever develop a taste for the stuff. One nervous swallow of it, neat and unpleasantly warm from being pressed up against a backside in someone's hip pocket, would leap back up the gullet instantly as if it had been caster oil. It had to be capped and forced back down again by huge, convulsive muscular bunchings of the throat – all causing the eyes to stream and the face to flush violently.

"God, that's great stuff," you would wheeze in a thin extruded voice that struggled to escape through the constricted passage of inflamed throat tissue.

Whisky could bring unexpected dangers too. A school pal of mine from Invermoriston, Duncan MacDonald, suggested at a suitable point during one of these dances that we head off down the road to where the Invermoriston bus was parked. He had put his half bottle on to the luggage rack, and it was time for a pull at it. We hauled back the sliding door and clambered into the chilly interior. There were no rustlings or fumblings from the darkness, so we were on our own. Not that that mattered too much really. Duncan felt along the rack and a grunt told me that he'd found it. He took a long swig and handed it on to me. I tilted back my head. Get it down and over with and doing its work as quickly as possible. Instantly, I knew that something was terribly wrong. I've already mentioned that my metabolism identified whisky as something alien and to be rejected. This was quite different. This was not a taste – this was an invasion of pure evil. By amazing luck, none of it went down my throat, but all of it was hurled out by huge volcanic spasms. I was just able to make out that Duncan was in a similar extreme state. He was hanging over a seat and racked with the same violent convulsions. Neither of us could utter a word but eventually just fell out of the bus and lay, literally, across the yielding branches of a nearby mass of bushes. Both of us were gripped by a feeling of terror. The abominable aftertaste brought on wave after wave of uncontrollable sickness. I have no idea now how long this lasted, but when we eventually staggered to our feet and looked at each other we had the same burning question: what in the name of God had we just tried to drink? Clearly it wasn't whisky. We found the bottle and there was the answer. It was brake fluid. Someone told me later that if we had swallowed a gulp of that, it could have been fatal. I have no idea if that is so, but it was only the alert throat muscles that saved me that night. For many years after this episode, I could still call up a memory of the sensation – not taste - that had so shattered my senses that night.

Violence of the more conventional drink-fuelled kind was never very far below the surface at these dances. Individuals who were normally meek and inoffensive would be seen hurling out challenges and blood would flow from noses and cut faces. The unspoken rule was that this sort of thing took place outside the hall – very rarely happening inside. On one occasion I managed to arouse the rage of the oldest of a large family who lived at the foot of Bunoich Brae, not far from our house. Hughie was big and bulky with short fair hair. He also had a short fuse when the fumes of alcohol rose to his brain and he could rapidly be transformed into a raging beast. Any shape that swam into his slow, red glare was a challenge that goaded him to attack. No other reason was necessary. On this occasion mine was that unfortunate shape. He lunged at me somewhere outside in the darkness when I was heading back into the warmth and noise after my swig from a half-bottle. I thought I could outrun him but soon he was right behind me. His hot alcohol breath surged all around me as he cursed and raved, bellowing what he was going to do to me. It was now getting scary. Here my common sense deserted me: instead of hurling myself towards the entrance into the actual dance hall and letting the doorkeepers deal with Hughie and his ravings, I turned sharp right, into the gents' cloakroom, charged into the toilet cubicle and slammed and bolted the door. Safe, I foolishly thought. The first monstrous blow on the door quickly told me otherwise. Hughie was now in full flight from whatever senses he might have had remaining and kick after kick began to bend the door inwards alternating with the dead-weight impacts of his full bulk. It wouldn't take very much more of this and I realised that my life-expectancy was pretty minimal. The insane howlings from the other side continued and then, with a final splintering, the door fell in on top of me followed by the still frenzied Hughie. I was saved at this moment by the appearance of a few who had seen what was happening. They launched themselves at my crazed attacker and eventually pinned him down where he could do no further harm. Even as I was picking myself out of the wreckage of the shattered door, Hughie was sliding back into oblivion.

A more harmless drunken episode stands out – this time where I was only an onlooker. During the War years, in keeping with national emergency regulations, the village hall had to have its windows covered with blackout screens. For quite a few years after the War was over, for some reason, some of these screens had not been thrown away, but were just left, propped up against one of the walls at the rear of the hall. They didn't get in the way of anybody and I suppose people just stopped seeing them any more. One night, there was an especially violent eightsome reel in progress, when a girl was sent spinning out of one of the sets and crashed into one of the screens. It went flying, and revealed a normally respectable member of the community. He was in a state of sagging drunkenness and standing in the characteristic pose of the human male relieving himself up against a wall. He turned his slow glazed eyes towards the massed surge of dancers who had just seen him as the horror of it all began to dawn on him. Next he fled into the night and much subsequent ridicule.

My most searing experience in those days didn't happen in Fort Augustus hall, but six miles to the east in Invermoriston village hall. It was an episode in which I lost face, dignity and any reputation I might have had up till then. It happened during my student days. My girl friend was staying with me during a holiday. We had gone, with a crowd of others, off down to Invermoriston to go to the Saturday night dance. Now, a brief reminder of the times in which this dance was taking place to fill in the background, as it were. This was the late fifties and Invermoriston, even more than Fort Augustus, could have been considered as sort of frontier country. Two massive dams were being built then up Glenmoriston – one quite far to the west at Cluanie and the other nearer one at Dundreggan. Each of these schemes had hundreds of workmen living in the primitive camps provided for them. These included the famous "Tunnel Tigers" – men whose lungs were lined with tunnel dust and who had fairly short life expectancies. Many of these men were poised to use much of their huge pay-packets to squeeze the maximum pleasure out of the weekend and where more obvious than the local pub and dance hall. Then there were the other men who worked in the forests, felling timber and dragging it out under contract to the Forestry Commission. These were dark, resin-impregnated men of basic, primitive urgings and appetite.

The dance was well under way. The small hall was packed and the fiddle and accordion were working hard. I was moving round the floor holding my girlfriend as we negotiated a waltz.

I felt a tap on my shoulder.

"Excuse me, pal," a voice grunted.

These were the days of the "Excuse Me" waltz. You could go up to any couple on the floor, tap the man on the shoulder, say, "excuse me" and waltz away with his partner. The only thing, this had to be announced beforehand by the MC. In the second it took me to watch my girlfriend vanishing into the mob, in the grasp of another, it hit me that no such announcement had been made.

I pushed through the heaving mass to where my girlfriend was being held ever more tightly by a relatively short but very squat and powerful man of the forests. His shirt was of bold check; he had ex-army trousers and wore his work boots. Also there was a powerful smell of resin from him that probably had soaked into his very bone marrow.

"Excuse me," I said.

I was totally ignored. Resin Man had no intention of letting my girlfriend go. I was beginning to feel a bit disturbed. Now it was time to turn up the temperature a little. A little more truculence.

"Look. It wasn't an 'excuse me'. You had no right…"

"F**k off," rumbled Resin Man and disappeared into the mass once again.

Now I was facing a full-blown crisis. I'm at a dance with my girlfriend whom I want to impress and I can't rescue her from the attentions of a man who is actually shorter than I am. It would have been bad enough if he had bulked over me. I shoved my way through the packed bodies yet again until I was right up behind them. He really had her held fast now, and she was starting to get a bit anxious herself. Resin Man was unmoved. Another pivot on his heavy boots took the pair of them right to the very centre of the dance floor. The shame was becoming corrosive. And even more public.

Then it was that I had one of those disastrous flashes of inspiration that can occur in life and which make a bad situation even more calamitous. Somewhere I had read in an article about self-defence that if you wanted to deal with someone who had you in forceful grasp and you wished to break it, all you had to do to loosen the villain's grip was to grasp one of his little fingers and bend it back sharply. Being the weakest finger, this would present no problem. The attacker would have to let go or run the risk of having the finger broken. So went the theory.

I loomed over my tormenter again.

"For the last time, let go. I'm warning you."

"Warning me? I told you to f**k off. Now do it."

I gripped one of the little fingers digging into my girlfriend's back.

"Right. You asked for this."

And I hauled at the finger, bracing myself for some violent reaction. A shout at least or even a blow coming at me. Anything - anything would be better than this very public humiliation.

I have to point out here that these men of the forests were not like the rest of us. They did a daily job that involved physical effort on a scale that few of the rest of could even imagine. One of the results of this was that they had muscles in places where we would just have flaccid tissue. Even little fingers could be crooked to lift heavy weights. And this was why I was totally unable to move either of those little fingers by as much as a millimetre. In fact, they were digging into my girlfriend even tighter and I was being dragged around the floor in utter ignominy. This was now very serious and I was being overwhelmed by the shame of it all. I was now attracting more and more of the puzzled stares of the other dancers. All seemed to be lost.

My saviour on that dreadful evening was a workmate from the hydro scheme where I had a job that holiday. He was the MC at the dance. He was vast and bearded. All that was required was a nod from him and a gesture towards the door for Resin Man to release my girlfriend and hunch his way off the floor.

She may now have been back at my side, but the whole evening was totally ruined. The male ego is a delicate thing and is not designed for that sort of savaging. Mine took a very long time to recover.

Of course these village dances were more than the extremes of primness and crudity that I originally suggested. They were a snapshot of most of the community at play and at its mating rituals. I do have to say "most" of the community since there was a code about who actually went to these functions. For instance, neither of my parents really approved of them. All the more odd in that for many years, my mother actually played in a local dance band that frequently provided the music. But for either of them actually to attend a dance was quite unthinkable. There was a sort of clear class divide in the village in those days. You had the ministers in their respective huge manses. Obviously you could count them out. There was the bank manager – also in his splendid house – and the local hotel proprietor. The local doctor and the proprietors of the local grocers' shops and sundry other business people, as well as any landowners, would never be found among the crowds who gathered in that bare Spartan hall at the top of Bunoich Brae. And there was another notable feature of these dances – they were not solely for the teenagers and those in their twenties: there was a fair mixture of older generations present as well and they mixed easily.

The dances we did were exclusively of the Scottish Dancing variety. They allowed a modicum of physical contact as well as being an outlet for the more violent undercurrents. During the Eightsome Reel, for example, the "birling" of the females could reach quite dangerous levels and even the slightly more douce "Strip the Willow" could have the girls cannoning off the other dancers as they were flung around to satisfy some part of the rutting instinct. Most were fairly simple – like the St Bernard's Waltz which was no more than a walk round the floor while the girl did all the work. Whenever something from the more obscure reaches of the Scottish Dance canon was announced, that was when the half bottle became a better prospect.

As I already mentioned, what violence there was took place outside the hall, though I do remember an exception to this. It happened during the final preparations for a Strip the Willow. The MC was doing his usual shouting to get more people on to the floor to make up the numbers and to get the whole unwieldy mass organised. The band was making the usual preparatory noises and I looked to my right at the stranger who was standing there. He had a slight sway that told me he was drunk, but not very much so. He was totally nondescript and non-menacing. I casually mentioned that it was hot in the hall and I was going to take off my jacket. This was the trigger for a stream of standard oaths and before I could even raise a hand to defend myself, he had landed a blow on the side of my head and followed that up with a further flurry to my lower regions. I was now on the floor and the kicks were beginning to hurt and it was not before time that help arrived on the scene from the doorkeepers and the frenzied stranger was dragged outside. I have no further recollections about this strange episode – who he was and what happened to him: all lost in the past. I suppose I could be forgiven if I had developed a bit of a persecution complex.

Then there was that primness that I referred to. For all the seethings of adolescent lust that were obviously there in that village dance hall, the chances of things going beyond a dance with any of the girls present were pretty remote. Certainly the notion of picking up a casual partner and having sex with her was a totally unreal (however much desired) outcome. The reasons are not too complex. In such a small community there was among the girls an over-riding fear of "losing reputation" even if they were to hint at a more relaxed attitude towards such matters. Taboos were strong and frightening and any who broke the code could suffer. Many of us could look at such a girl with an uneasy speculation but it was not easy to take the matter much further. One such was one of a brother and sister pair from a neighbouring village. He was drunk from the moment he entered the hall to the point, usually fairly early in the proceedings, when he would collapse like a disjointed puppet. His suit had an odd sheen about it that was the result of the accumulation of the wax he had picked up from his rolling on the floors of the various dance halls he had visited. His sister had a reputation for easy availability, but it was just too dangerous. Any approach would have found its way back to the parental ear at some point. There was no censure on behavioural patterns quite as effective as that of the small community looking after its own. My father was local headmaster and my mother was also a teacher, so the very notion of crossing that border was beyond consideration. Only if drink had been consumed beyond the manageable level, of course. Lust, it has to be said, went for the most part unassuaged. To sum it all up, these dances for the adolescent male were a vast amount of yearning, a certain amount of permitted contact in the well-lit dance hall and, if very, very lucky, a modicum of fumbling in the darkness outside. Things were to improve immeasurably in my late teens when I had passed my driving test in the family 1939 SS Jaguar. This black, heavy machine with its flaring chrome radiator and enormous headlamps was a formidable addition to my hitherto feeble armoury. The usual strictures on female comportment were still in place but with the environment being upgraded so dramatically, a little of that lustful pounding could be eased.

There was another constraint on contacts with the opposite sex in my village in those days and that was religion. Fort Augustus is overshadowed by the huge bulk of the Benedictine Abbey (abandoned by that Order in 1998). Its two towers looked down on us all – one with its slow-chiming clock that we all depended upon and the other, the pointed one with its large bells that would ring at strange times to mark mysterious points in the Catholic calendar. As well as being the home to a community of Benedictine monks, it also housed a boys' boarding school and a large church that was the focal point for Catholic worship for much of the Great Glen. Incidentally, in those days, the boys in the Abbey school were permitted absolutely no contact with the outside community. They were a strange sight to us in their scarlet blazers with the badge of the black crow on the breast pocket. They played cricket and rugby – games that we associated with stories of English boarding schools. In effect as far as we were concerned, they could have come from another planet.

Across the village, to the north of the Abbey and on its own small hill, stood the Free Church – stark and narrow-windowed. It glared across at its implacable foe at the head of the loch, where it bulked in all its might of carved stone and stained glass, and fulminated regularly against the baneful influence of Rome. Then there was the Church of Scotland. It was sited to the west and was also on its plot of raised ground. It was less censorious of the Abbey and all it stood for but the awareness of difference was always in the air. I was Church of Scotland, though my father – as is mentioned elsewhere – had been brought up in the Free Church but had abandoned it a few years previously. Now it would be all too easy with this triangular religious distribution to conclude that my home village had seething tensions just below the surface that would occasionally erupt into something more serious. Not so. These things were much more circumspect in the village. At the local dances, the choice of partner who might be from the other camp meant no more than the attraction of the moment. Behind it, though, was the pretty certain knowledge that that was as far as it was likely to go. Any marriage across the divide would be the occasion for head-shaking and "no good will come of it" asides. It was very rare and just was in the category of "not done". But no riots broke out nor were stones hurled through windows in the night. It was all very civilised. It was not till a few years later that I was struck with the first shock waves of the reality of Scotland's shameful sectarian divides. My home village in those days thought nothing of the sight of a Church of Scotland sale in the MacKay Hall where several of the helping women would be Catholic. It's just the way it happened and nobody seemed to give it a second thought. Apart from the disapproval of the mixed marriage - and always in my recollection it was based mainly on the notion that any offspring would have to be brought up in the Catholic faith irrespective of the wishes of the non-Catholic partner - apart from that exception, there was little or no tension or animosity between the faiths in the life of the villagers in Fort Augustus in those days.

The attitudes of society to alcohol and driving have changed hugely since the fifties. I can still break out into a sheen of cold sweat if I think back to the state in which I found myself behind the wheel of the family car when heading to or from a dance in those days. How could my parents, normally so precise in their attitude to social mores, not have suspected what might have been going on on these nights when I had swung BCX 909 (the Jaguar) or its even more dashing successor, HUY 807, the one-and-a-half litre Riley out of the garage and pointed it down Bunoich Brae? Probably the luck that had never the slightest dent or scratch appear on either car was enough to convince that my behaviour was always impeccable. In this area, there was what can only be called a communal blindness. Having a drink before going behind the wheel really lacked the stigma that it has nowadays. One incident will illustrate. I had headed across the village in the big, black, shiny Jaguar to pick up some pals and had forced down several nauseous gulps of whisky. It set about its deadly business quicker than usual so that by the time I was heading back to the hall, I was having problems with focussing on the road ahead. I was approaching the foot of Bunoich Brae where the road heaved almost vertically up left from the main road. Even in normal sober circumstances it was rather a difficult manoeuvre in those days. The gear-box in a pre-War Jaguar was an unforgiving piece of equipment. The lower gears lacked the modern decadence of synchromesh so that the double-de-clutch had to be called upon to change down. The tiniest slip, and you could find yourself in a nightmare of flayed metal and shredded dignity. And that was what happened as I was hauling the huge bonnet round to point the chrome radiator up the brae: I spectacularly missed first gear. As I was wrestling with the juddering gear lever and trying to keep some control, I saw a blaze of headlights bearing down on me. Something huge and unstoppable was just about to make contact. Instinctively, I depressed the clutch pedal and the Jaguar fell back on to the main road again – directly into the path of another set of blazing headlights that swerved and lurched violently on to the grassy verge. Angry voices were crackling and bellowing all around me – from the terrified passengers and the enraged drivers who had been given a severe fright. But the main memory I carry with me is that it wasn't the fact that I was clearly unfit to be in charge of a car that caused the rage – it was the fact that I had shown total ineptitude behind the wheel. No suggestion that I might be reported to the police or anything even occurred to anyone.

Earlier mention of the nearby Free Church Manse brings the final snapshot of these dances. The Free Church minister in those days, Reverend MacLeod, was as stern and dark a figure as ever preached a stern and dark sermon from a pulpit. His wife was large and carried her own disapproving air. Between them, they had brought into the world a son, Hector, who was to move in and out of our lives until we lost contact with him completely after 1958. It requires little imagination to picture his parents' response to him asking if he could go to a dance whose noise and flickering movements could be heard and seen tantalisingly and dangerously close over the wall that ran around the extensive manse grounds. Hector had the answer though, and we were a part of his master plan. When it was dark enough, I, my brother and sundry others would carry a long and heavy ladder from one of the manse sheds. We would wait for Hector to signal from his bedroom window that all was clear. Next we heaved the ladder into place, and he would shin down to take advantage of several hours of freedom in the dance hall – which he would use to spectacular effect. He was one of that favoured few who had little problem in the mating business. And, yes, I did savagely envy him. It sounds so improbable to recount this now, but he actually got away with this on all of the occasions that he fled his prison. No parent ever checked that he was still in his bedroom after he had bidden goodnight. To get back into the Manse he needed our help again.

The ladder was a heavy one and had to be stored back in its shed afterwards.

Vehicles I Have Known

BCX 909

The thrill of being in charge of a car or a lorry while still in one's teens is all too obvious, but in my case it was all the more so in that opportunities in the fifties were much more scarce. I was fortunate in that ours was a car-owning household, something that was far from common then. Not only that, both I and my brother had managed to pass our driving tests while still in school: something even more rare. There was no driving school in Fort Augustus, but there was one excellent source of learning the skills. His name was "Ikie" Campbell and he was one of the local postmen. He was prepared to take adolescents like me out in a car on a regular basis, and to teach all the tricks required to pass the driving test. It was a formidable test in those days too. Ikie's patience was legendary, and many were the times he sat in the passenger seat of the mighty Jaguar (already referred to) and led me through the subtleties of smooth gear-changes in a pre-war gearbox, the emergency stop and reversing into a narrow opening. Long runs to Inverness I also recollect as well as nightmarish hill-starts on the almost vertical Bunoich Brae. Then of course, there was the dramatic Emergency Stop. This instruction went on, in my case, for many weeks and I have to admit with utter shame something that has haunted me over the past half century since then. It is the fact that Ikie never charged a penny for his tutoring and after I had passed the test (first time too!) I never got around to offering him a gift of some kind for all his extraordinary patience and skill. For some reason or other, it never occurred to me. Even at this late date, I can only apologise.

The very first thing I did when the silent, grey driving examiner handed me my magical pass certificate (green, I think?) was, naturally, to whip off the L plates. Then before going up to the schoolhouse and bragging to my parents, I headed west out of the village to what we then knew as the "Straight Mile". This stretch of road, obviously straight, was just beyond Loch Unagan and before Aberchalder. It was a little bit short of a mile actually, but it was a marvellous stretch of the highway on which to let loose the full potential of the vehicle. And that's what I did. The ever-cautious Ikie would never allow me to go over the speed limit by so much as a whisker, but now I was free of all that. I pointed the long black bonnet with its chrome cap at the end along the ribbon of road and pressed the accelerator down hard. A pre-War car – even one as prestigious as a Jaguar – was rather slow to get the message when the spurs were being dug in, so that it was getting towards the end of the "Mile" and the first curve to be got round that the speed was nudging eighty miles an hour. Remember too that cars in those days were so different from today. Each had its own sly quirks and tricks that a driver had to learn. The steering was often loose and required constant adjustment by the driver even to keep a straight line and brakes were primitive and slow in their response. I was in a state of almost terror as I saw the end of the Straight Mile rushing towards me and began to pump the brakes desperately. They began to grip in time to let me hurl the Jaguar into the turn and manage to keep to my own side of the road. I was in a state of turmoil as I pulled into a lay-by and sat gripping the wheel and gasping. It had been exhilarating but quite terrifying. I was in a rather more subdued mood as I turned the Jaguar around and drove back to the village rather more sedately and headed home to receive the family plaudits.

The possession of a driving licence was a huge achievement – a magic passport to many opportunities. I was still a pupil in Glenurquhart Secondary School and the school Christmas Dance was one occasion when I could really make that impression that all young men craved. I had as passengers, as I recollect, my brother, sister and my sister's closest friend Theresa. Off we set – with full parental approval – down the snaking, dark road by Loch Ness side. How could parents have been so trusting? All went without hitch until I was negotiating the twists on a steep hill some five miles to the west of Lenie. I swept round a corner and saw on the road ahead and picked out starkly in the headlights, a large black jagged piece of the beetling rock face on my left that had broken free. No chance of swerving or braking and the car went directly over it. The jolt, crunch and crack from underneath spoke of serious damage. The exhaust had been ruptured so that the full bellowing of the unsilenced engine began to batter our ears. No matter how slowly I went or how light the pressure on the accelerator that dreadful racket now dominated an already ruined evening. My schoolmates whom I had hoped to impress guffawed hugely at our ignominious arrival, as we pulled up outside Blairbeg Hall in a shattering cacophony. And they were there to see us roaring off into the night when we headed back home on the nightmare return journey. Not even the most head-turning car on earth can look dignified with a burst exhaust. I can also recollect the noise of part of the collapsed system as it dragged on the road underneath, little aware of the deadly danger of fire from the inevitable showers of sparks that would have been thrown out so close to the petrol tank.

This car shared one feature with all the ones that my father bought: it stood out from the rest around it. In the thirties, he drove that most raffish of vehicles, an open-topped, red MG Sports car with wire wheels and huge steering wheel. During the War years he had a dark green Triumph Gloria which none of us ever really enjoyed, since it only ever left its garage on Home Guard business. Then came the Jaguar. He had seen it advertised in some motor magazine. New cars were very scarce in the early fifties so the second-hand market flourished. The Jaguar was being sold by a garage in London, so my father paid the local garage owner, Ian Grant, to travel down to London, give the car a look-over and if it seemed all right, to then drive it back north to Fort Augustus. Excitement built up as we awaited its arrival and I can still sense the amazement when the huge chrome radiator with its equally impressive headlights swept up into the playground behind the schoolhouse. This great black gleaming thing was now ours. It was a complete disaster. I often feel that Ian was astute enough when he gave BCX 909 its look-over in London, with Arthur Daley's stepfather looking on, to realise that this impressive-looking car would provide him with a plentiful and regular income for years to come. And that was what happened: it spent much of its life up on the ramp in Ian's garage. Apart from transmission problems, it had obviously been left out in all weathers for long spells so that water had seeped in to warp the splendid walnut fascia on the passenger side. This damp had had a dire effect on the electrics too so that there were frequent major breakdowns. One dreadful family adventure will illustrate this. We had set out to drive to Edinburgh to stay with the Birketts in Cluny Drive in Morningside. This was truly about our favourite holiday destination for many happy reasons. We intended to call in at the Millers at Laggan Bridge where my uncle Dave had the shop there. He was married to my mother's younger sister, Annie. This meant that the first part of our long journey took us along Loch Lochy side. As we were driving along, the horn began to make sporadic little bleeps. They became more and more frequent and then became a full-throated braying. Other motorists began to show signs of irritation and puzzlement at this seemingly arrogant car that appeared to be wanting to shoulder aside every other road user. Spean Bridge wasn't too far away and there was a garage there that could have a look at the problem. But there was more to come. It was then that the headlights began to flash on and off. Some of the oncoming drivers would helpfully point and toot their horns to draw my father's attention but this made him even more enraged so that he would sometimes lean out of the window and bellow "I know, I know!" as he forged on. Inside the car there was a grim mixture of humiliation and dread, not helped by my mother – who was always the worst passenger on earth – who was making matters even worse with her doom-laden running commentary. Lights and horn were duly fixed at Spean Bridge and on we continued. When we were well down the road to Edinburgh, the faulty wiring struck once again. The rain that had been threatening began to crash down. The wipers on the old Jaguar were activated by pulling out a knurled, chrome knob in front of the driver and passenger. This activated the wiper motor and engaged the actual blade itself to begin its sweep. Except that it didn't. The motor remained silent and the windscreen was streaming with water. I was made to go into the front passenger seat and to lean across in front of my now-simmering father and manually work the wiper in front of him for most of the rest of that journey from hell. The effort required was quite appalling, mainly because of the sheer awkwardness of reaching the thing and bouts of cramp just added to the misery. But the absolute necessity of keeping that windscreen clear enough for my father to drive the car had me twist the thing for mile after dreadful mile. I seem to recollect that the rain did eventually ease and I was able to relax enough to experience the adventure of crossing the Forth by the huge ferry that plied the firth at Queensferry in those days. There was one more jarring episode in that blighted journey before we got to the longed-for destination at 24 Cluny Drive in Morningside. In those days, the undisputed king of the streets of Edinburgh was the tram. It ran on its complex rail system and was not really very motorist friendly in that it was unable to steer but had to keep to its prescribed course. My father had his navigation worked out as to how to get to Morningside and it involved, at some point, Morrison Street. Morrison Street failed to co-operate in this plan and we found ourselves in the middle of some nightmare intersection of interweaving tram lines with several of these tall, maroon and cream towers looming over us. Our car was effectively blocking their way. My frantic father was calling out hoarsely to a uniformed Edinburgh Transport functionary "Can you tell me how to get to Morrison Street?" Directions must have been forthcoming since we eventually made it to the leafy calm of Cluny Drive

This episode might go a little way to explaining the strange paradox involved in my father's relationship with his cars. Although he always wanted to own models that stood out from the common herd, he actually didn't like driving all that much. In fact, from the moment I passed my test he was all too willing to sit in the front passenger seat and let me get on with it. Maybe it was my mother who was partly to blame for this. I have already mentioned the doleful running commentary that filled the uneasy air as the various systems in the car were breaking down. Her devastating presence in the car – especially when my father was behind the wheel – was probably based on her experience earlier in her marriage when she had agreed to let my father give her driving lessons. It seems that their marriage survived that crucible of pain and humiliation, but only just. But it meant that from that date on, she could never be comfortable or silent while he was driving. Her comments were not shrill or strident. It was much worse. It was a small voice intoning the brief "Aren't you going too fast for this corner?" right through to the confidence-shattering "I think I'll have to ask you to stop and let me off right here!" Certainly she could reduce the car interior to a seething cauldron of tensions for all of us. A later chapter will illustrate this forcefully enough.

After the Jaguar had gone, it was no ordinary, everyday car that replaced it. That wasn't the way my father did things. One of the car sales rooms in Inverness provided just what he wanted. I even swear that I heard him telling my mother that the Riley he wanted to buy had been in the possession of an elderly lady from Spean Bridge who had kept for most of its life in the garage and had a hired driver to take it out on the road on its rare excursions. It certainly did have a remarkably low mileage, but no matter what its true provenance, it was one truly magnificent and head-turning vehicle in those days of fifties dull, lumpen car design. Our Riley looked spectacularly rakish with its gleaming red bodywork, black leather-covered roof and wooden fascia with elegant instruments. It also had a chrome-framed split panel windscreen and expensive red leather upholstery. It even had two extra headlights fitted. Yes, people noticed when the Riley was in town.

I have to admit to being amazed at the ease with which my father could be persuaded to let me take the car for a spin in the spring or summer evenings. Soon there were two other cars that joined me as others of my friends passed their tests too. First of all, Ally Matheson. He was the son of the proprietor of Inchnacardoch Hotel, which was about a mile out of the village to the east. Its spacious, comfortable red sandstone presence stood on the edge of the dark Forestry trees and at the end of a sweeping driveway. Mr Matheson had a black Austin saloon and his son Ally was a supremely proficient driver of it. He had had years of experience on that hotel driveway long before he was old enough for his provisional licence. The other of this local youthful elite was Hector MacLeod, the son of the Free Church minister – already a somewhat raffish presence in these reminiscences. In an act so totally out of character for a dark-suited representative of the more extreme Presbyterian persuasion, the Reverend MacLeod suddenly appeared in a brand-new, gleaming, two-tone grey and maroon Ford Consul. As well as the amazing bench seats in the front and the soft undulating suspension, it had that icon of fifties motoring chic – the steering column gear lever. Being owner of a brand-new vehicle would naturally have made Reverend MacLeod cautious about letting his son drive around the village on his own but his place as minister in the sternest of the village churches made it well-nigh impossible for Hector to get hold of it at all – officially, that is. This was merely a challenge to such an archetypical son of the manse. Luckily for Hector, the garage where the gleaming new machine was housed was about a couple of hundred yards away from the manse. It was a substantial, barn-like building and it was also hidden by trees and a high wall from the ministerial study window. So it became just a matter of sneaking the keys when no-one was looking and it was off down Bunoich Brae for a whirl round the village. Now, this combination of Hector and the new Ford Consul with its seductive bench seat at the front was pretty effective combination for the pursuit of village talent and it has to be said his easy skill in this department had many of us more than a bit envious. So it was that the Great Practical Joke was set up. Ally Matheson's father was a special constable and had the full police uniform at home all the time. Ally sneaked it out one night when we knew that Hector had an assignation and would be sure to drive along the back road to the village – the Bruich Dhubh. We lay in wait for him concealed and, sure enough, the Consul oozed its way over the small hump-backed bridge heading for the dark tunnel of the aptly-named Brae. The headlight beam on the black Austin leaped ahead and with Ally in his police uniform at the wheel, we soon were close behind Hector and his shadowy companion. A flashing of the headlight beam and he drew fearfully into the side. We had the indescribable but cruel delight of watching the utterly convincing police constable in diced cap and shiny-buttoned tunic leaning into the jerkily-opening driver's window, uttering the dread words, "Could I see your driving licence, Sir?"

I'm sure we all laughed together about it some time later but even recounting the episode brings a slight tremor of guilt at the rather nasty trick we played that night.

There was an intense rivalry between the Riley and the Matheson Austin. The only snag about all the Riley's late forties luxury (it was a 1949 model) was the weight of the body in relation to the power output of the engine. It has to be admitted that its performance wasn't all that impressive. This was an unpalatable fact that the Matheson Austin regularly had us face up to on the regular dashes up the fearsome twists of Glendoe Brae on the south side of Loch Ness beyond the village. The idea was to see which car could get furthest up the Brae in the highest gear. No matter how fiercely the Riley was hurled at the Glendoe Brae, it was always the Austin that could sustain top gear for ages then dropping into third and still puttering on when the Riley was forced quickly down into second. It was truly galling but nothing could be done about it – except to feel a sense of "noblesse oblige" from behind the wheel of what was still a luxury car and not a tinny, mass-produced Austin saloon.

It was a trip to Inverness in the Riley that has been etched in my mind forever as perhaps the most cringingly embarrassing experience of my driving life. And that includes up till the present day. I was driving, of course. My father was in the front seat while my mother was in the back. We were heading home to Fort Augustus after some errands in the town had been completed. Everything was calm and routine and I was looking forward to the drive along the loch side as well as the call in at Drumnadrochit for a cup tea at my grandmother's. All was well with the world. We were moving up Inglis Street towards what was known in those days as "Boot's Corner" - for the obvious reason that Boots the Chemist used to occupy the main building there. We were going to turn right at the traffic lights there and head down High Street, then Bridge Street – over the bridge and off along Glenurquhart Road and the road west to Fort Augustus. But something was afoot in the town. The movement of the people on the pavements and a sense of something intangible in the air spoke of unusual events unfolding. Sealed off from all this inside the Riley, we only got an impression; neither had any of us read anything in the local press that would have warned us. I did notice, though, that the traffic lights up ahead were not working. I nosed gingerly on to High Street and saw at once that it was totally empty of traffic. And the pavements on both sides were crammed with huge crowds of people craning to look somewhere back over our heads and in the opposite direction to the one we were heading. It was clear now that they were expecting something spectacular to happen and clearly it was not the appearance of a red, black-roofed Riley that was now so stunningly and appallingly in a place where it had no right to be.

A policeman was leaning over the bonnet of the car and banging on it with his fist.

He was puce with rage and he was mouthing various things that I couldn't make out. I was wrestling with the handle to lower the window, but it sounded like, "Back up! Back up!" The window was stuck and took a few seconds to get it open enough for me to hear what was going on. It was then I made out what sounded like, "God, it's too late!"

He directed the full blast of his fury at me again.

"Get up on to the kerb. Right now. As far as you can. NOW!"

But already his apoplectic instructions were being drowned out by a powerful wave of bagpipe music that was rolling towards us from Eastgate. The largest pipe band in the world with a vast forest of prickly bayonets following closely behind, was swinging purposefully towards us – and we were directly in its path. We were stuck there at the narrowest part of the street.

Only now did the full horror really crash down upon me. I tried to make myself shrink and effectively disappear.

Just try to grasp the sheer awfulness of our situation – or I should say MY situation. I was, after all, the driver. That whole huge procession made up of pipers, drummers, officers, other ranks – all of them had to close in significantly to get past the bulk of the Riley. This was no small modern car. The tide of uniformed humanity seemed to go on and on and on. It was the longest military procession in the history of the Highlands and still it squeezed in and swung out again to head towards a saluting dais set up a few hundred yards further down the High Street, outside the Town Hall.

The final clenching embarrassment came from the fact that we were receiving abuse from the unfortunates who had picked that spot to get the best view, only to have the uncompromising bulk of our car stuck right in front of them. They made their, often pungent, views very clear.

Now, this truly awful episode lay locked away deep in my psyche for many, many years. Then, one day, I happened on one of these "Old Inverness in Pictures" publications. I was idly turning the pages when a deep churning in the entrails of my innermost self occurred. That place where the most secret memories are stored.

I was looking at a photo taken from a high vantage point to the west of the area outside the Town House – on the Bridge Street side. In the foreground was a raised dais with sundry dignitaries in robes of office and one or two high-ranking military types. The camera's eye took in the full sweep of the High Street and showed a large military pipe band marching along it, followed by a mass of soldiery in kilts and spats and all with rifles with bayonets fixed. The shutter had clicked at the moment the officers at the head were turning to salute the dais with its complement of the Great and the Good. I was becoming drenched in cold sweat, as I looked more closely up the length of the street in that old photo. I was searching for the Riley. But of its embarrassing bulk at Boot's Corner there was no sign whatsoever. Only the mass of tiny faces of the crowds, the proud regiment and the diced caps of the Highland's Finest – the local constabulary. We were nowhere to be seen.

I began then to puzzle over this. All the evidence as I studied that photograph seemed to suggest that I was looking at that event involving HUY 807 with its cringing occupants and their straying so inappropriately on to a huge public stage. But we were not there. I just let the matter rest there – only vaguely speculating on the possibility that the authorities of the town of Inverness when they saw our apparent failed attempt to ruin a solemn civic occasion, had, in the manner of the old Soviet Union when it wished to alter pictorial history by simply airbrushing their non-persons out of the picture, had had us similarly erased.

As a brief footnote, I cannot locate a photo of a military parade in the town around 1960 that would fit the details of my memory. The nearest I have found is one dated 1961 (and that could have been the year I have been talking about). This photo shows the Cameron Highlanders crossing the temporary bridge over the River Ness on their last march through the town before they were amalgamated with the Seaforths. But these soldiers all seem to be wearing dark tunics and I am pretty certain that the ones that must have silently cursed us as we forced them to squeeze up at Boot's Corner were wearing khaki. It all must remain a mystery now. It would be nice to know, though, if there is in someone's album somewhere, a picture of the Riley that almost disrupted that regiment's march through the town of Inverness.

KST 486

As I've mentioned earlier, of all the variety of jobs available for such as I in the fifties, the driving ones were far and away the best. At that time, the Forestry Commission was constructing roads in the hills above Invermoriston and Fort Augustus. These were lucrative times for local entrepreneurs who could get hold of pretty clapped-out old lorries (those were the days before MOT Certificates had ever been heard of) and let them loose on any of several contracts. All that was required was a young driver who would probably even pay you to let him drive your lorry and you had a nice little earner.

One of these go-ahead locals was Pat, the garage owner in Invermoriston. (Better known as "Pat the Pier"). Both my brother and I got jobs with him in the late fifties. Apart from the rickety state of some of his rolling stock, he was a good employer. Certainly the pay was better than most other jobs going then. I was excited at the prospect and only began to feel a sense of unease when Pat introduced me to my machine on the first morning. It was an ancient, short-wheelbase, petrol-driven Bedford. It was painted a vile, bilious green colour and among its most outstanding mechanical eccentricities was the piece of bent-over fence wire that poked up through a gap in the floor of the cab. You had to haul on this to activate the tipper when getting rid of your load.

The daily routine of my new job was straightforward enough. I would get a lift in one of the Hydro workers' buses in the early morning, which took me to Pat's garage. I would start up the Bedford and then head off up Glenmoriston to a place called Bhlaraidh. There I would leave the Glen road and heave my way up to the huge tip of tunnel spoil (material dug out from Hydro tunnels) where I would then reverse into position to have the Bedford loaded by a dumper truck driven by the most silent driver of any vehicle in the Highlands. We never exchanged anything more than the most perfunctory of grunts throughout all the weeks I spent on that job. After the last crash of the dumper's bucket upending its load of rocks and dust behind you, there followed the heavy, sagging, lurching progress back down to the road again on groaning springs and then the run back down the glen, three or four miles, till you reached the bottom end of the Forestry road. All holiday traffic was brushed aside, of course. My rusty hulk had precedence over all of these effete pleasure-seekers – and well they knew it.

Now, as it happened, this first morning's trip was to be the only one that I ever did with the bile-green Bedford. And this is what happened.

I swung wide to aim the stubby green bonnet up the rough, new Forestry road, changing into bottom gear for the fierce gradient. The elderly engine took on a desperate, near-hysterical note but it kept churning away. The gear lever leapt and my world became a raging torrent of the noise of metal components on the edge of self-destruction. Suddenly the steering wheel went slack. It began to spin uselessly. The perspective outside the cab began to shift alarmingly and I realised that I was slowly being lifted up. In fact, my cab was actually rearing like a stallion pawing the air. The load behind me was too heavy and the centre of gravity was moving dangerously. I managed to keep enough cool to slip the clutch and run swiftly back down to the main road. Saved – but I was shaking with fright.

Straight back to the garage at Invermoriston and a confrontation with Pat.

Pat was quite philosophical.

"All right. Come back tomorrow and I ought to have something better for you."

And he certainly did. It was good old KST 486 – a long-wheelbase Morris truck. The first big plus in KST's favour was that it was diesel. In the macho stakes, the heavy, sweaty throb of diesel was much more exciting than the thin whine of petrol. It was much bigger than the disgraced Bedford and looked more broad-shouldered and rugged. You could almost imagine the stubble on its chin. Cabs on commercial vehicles in those days were pretty rudimentary, but this one kept out wind and rain effectively. However there was one major snag – the starter motor had long packed in and had never been replaced. When Pat introduced my new lorry to me that morning, he showed me that it had been reversed into a narrow cul-de-sac off the main road beside one of the sheds adjoining his garage. The rear wheels were raised up high on a pile of old railway sleepers. That was how it had to be parked each night when the working day was over. The morning routine was as follows: climb into the cab and switch on the ignition. Wait a suitable length of time for things under the long bonnet to warm up and get primed. Then, wind down both of the cab windows and strain the ears to listen for any traffic from either direction. If all was silent and the road was clear, then the handbrake was released. The initial impetus from the raised rear wheels saw you across the road and heading towards the small, fairly steep brae that led down towards the old Invermoriston pier. A point was reached at the very cusp of the brae when the lorry almost stopped. You leaned forward and rocked yourself to urge it on at this point. Then it painfully picked up momentum until the clutch pedal could be released and the big crude engine could be forced into life. There would be the satisfaction then of racing the engine before turning at the foot of the brae and heading off up the glen with the roar of diesel power echoing around you. Even less chance for the holiday traffic when the huge bonnet of KST 486, like Desperate Dan's chin, was bearing down on them. It was all highly satisfactory.

I have a photograph that shows the rear view of a stubby, dull-looking lorry in the middle distance against the skyline. The driver's mirror on the long spindly arm of KST 486 and part of its front wing can be seen in the left foreground. Nothing in this picture contains the slightest element of impending danger or drama. You would be so wrong to think so. I had been the next lorry in line behind the one in the photo, awaiting my turn to move into position, turn around (it was slower for me because my lorry was longer that the rest working on this road), reverse up to the dumping point and then tip my load of crushed rock and stones where it would then be spread by bulldozer and shovel to make the rudimentary road surface. Since it happened to be my last day on this job, I wanted to take a photograph. I had brought with me my then pride and joy, my Voigtlander Perkeo One camera but I only had one exposure left on the film. I pointed it at the lorry just ahead before it moved off to get into position to tip its load. I got the correct range on the neat little range-finder, took a reading on the light exposure meter, sighted carefully through the Kontur-Finder (this was one complicated camera, let me tell you) then carefully pressed the shutter release.

Instead of the usual prim little "ping" it gave, I was shocked by a loud, ear-splitting crack. I was totally baffled. It came from the lorry I had just photographed.

At the precise second I had released the shutter on my camera, the rear, right-hand springs on the lorry had snapped with a report like a rifle. The whole vehicle tipped slowly and frighteningly towards the steep drop down the hillside to Invermoriston far below. And (echoes of the green Bedford) the cab rose grotesquely into the air. A wild flailing of limbs could just be seen through the rear cab window as the desperate driver flung open the door on the passenger side and leaped for his life. His lorry sagged further at the rear and then toppled slowly over the edge and down the slope. Its remains might lie there to this day.

KST 486, on two occasions, cautioned me against the sin of hubris I might have entertained at being able to pilot it on the relatively safe (well, fairly) roads up and down Glenmoriston and into the hills. I was reminded that it would take more than a few weeks at the wheel of a diesel truck to attain the real skills of a lorry driver. The first occasion occurred fairly early on in the job. I was on my way up to Bhlaraidh on the first run with the lorry empty. A fine sunny morning and the cab window was open. My arm was casually draped out of the window and the first fag of the morning dangled from my lip. Up ahead, I caught sight of a squad of Forestry workers who had just disembarked from their transport before heading into the hills to cut bracken or something. It happened that I knew quite a number of them and had worked with them on various occasions in the past. No more of that for me, though. I had the comfort of the cab and the thrill of the power of the big engine in the long bonnet out ahead of me. They were about to get a little demonstration to rub all this in for them. I was rapidly approaching a small humped bridge, which would require me to slow down. It would also require me to change down into third gear. Now, the gearbox in the Morris was not the worst I had even dealt with: another later tale will introduce you to that. But it was old, worn and tired – and demanded patience and a little respect. But I was about to give my demonstration and such thoughts were put aside. I was going to change down twice with double de-clutching, while giving a loud blare on the horn and a cheery wave as I swept past the lumpen crowd of labourers by the road side. Down into third gear I went with neatly timed clutch and accelerator. But instead of leaving it at that, I immediately went for the dip into second. And then it all went so spectacularly wrong. My timing failed and the glen reverberated to the drawn-out shriek of a tortured gearbox. I fought with the shuddering lever and was forced almost to a halt – right beside the bemused Forestry squad who had now realised who the red-faced, hunched figure in the cab was. Such humiliation. How I rued the folly of that second unnecessary gear change for many a long day after that.

The other sobering experience was a little more drawn-out – but was also very effective.

Pat had announced one day that instead of doing the tunnel-spoil run up the Glen, I was to go the next day to Fort William to collect a load of lime that was then to be delivered to a farm away at the top of Glen Moriston, somewhere beyond Torgoyl Bridge. This was excellent news. A long run up the Great Glen, westwards to Fort William, on a summer's day and one single load to deal with. I got all my directions as to how to find the limekiln and I set off in high spirits. The lime came from a works about a couple of miles on the Spean Bridge side of Fort William. It was easy enough to find and was fairly close to the main road. When I got there, I found that I'd have to reverse my lorry under a hopper standing on iron supports that didn't allow much space on either side. No real problem, I thought and began to edge carefully back, leaning out of the cab window. It was awkward that way, so I opened my door to get a better view of the manoeuvre. All seemed well, until a hideous crunching sound told me that something evil had happened. In shaving up close to the iron support on my side, I had forgotten that I had opened the door. It struck the grimly unrelenting support and crushed the door back into its hinges. When I moved forward again, I found that the door would no longer shut. It was now completely out of alignment. The utter shame of it all – to have made such a cretinous mistake on such a public stage. One of the staff at the kiln gave me some rope or wire to hold my door fast and I watched in misery as the cascade of white, dead-weight lime filled up the lorry and listened to the springs groan in their deep suffering.

The return trip was now to become a nightmare. First of all there was the frightening weight of the load I was now carrying. It seemed to be twice as heavy as the tunnel spoil and it affected the handling of KST severely. The lorry seemed to wallow on the road and the engine, normally robust and confident in tone, seemed to be on the point of giving up completely on some of the longer hills. It seemed to be uttering howls of protest when it was down to first gear and I was reduced to praying that it would make it up to and over the brow of yet another brae. In addition, I was now a total menace to all traffic coming up behind me and had queues of enraged fellow road-users who would shoot past me, sometimes with horns blaring in fury. Eventually, I reached Invermoriston and was left with the eight or nine miles up the Glen to the farm. What unutterable relief. Mind you, I still had to tell Pat that I'd damaged his lorry. Maybe I'd tell some lie that would cover up my clumsiness – but I didn't. More intense trauma lay ahead in the immediate future. The lorry groaned up the final mile to the farm gate I was to open to get to the field where the monstrous load was to be dumped. I could see a tractor moving about in the near distance as I was getting down to open the gate. Back into the cab and rev up the engine. Almost there. Bliss. But the pitiless weight of my accursed load was to have the last laugh. The rear wheels began to sink and all my efforts simply made matters worse. I could have leaned over the steering wheel and wept; the whole thing was now so humiliating at the end of a hateful day. It was as if gratuitous lashings of vile bad luck were being heaped on me. But help was to hand. The tractor appeared alongside and the driver – a stranger to me – had a cursory look at my predicament. In a blink of time he had a chain attached to my rear axle and the lorry was dragged out of its sucking, clinging mess. Before I could even mention that I still had the problem of getting the load of lime through the narrow gate and into the field, my saviour had offered to do it for me. I was pathetically grateful and could only look on in awe as he whirled my lorry round and, with appearing to take only a casual interest in what was happening behind him, he reversed the bulk of KST at top speed bang between the gate posts and then up to the precise spot where the load had to be tipped out.

I drove back down to Invermoriston a much sadder and indeed wiser driver than the one that had set out to the west on that sunny July morning of 1959.

Just when I thought I'd wound up my chapter on Pat the Pier, Glenmoriston and the road building schemes there, a stray inquiry of my brother (during my sporadic research) into his association with this local entrepreneur, brought to light another incident that I had totally forgotten. And an astonishing co-incidence too that makes it all the more startling to me that it should have disappeared from my memory so completely. Gregor, my younger brother, was also caught up in the risky thrills of driving heavy lorries – indeed his experiences were more adventurous than mine it has to be said. He had found himself in the cab of a truly frightening vehicle with the triumphalist banner "*Pride of the Glen*" emblazoned on its huge, creaking wooden cab. He was involved in the building of a road in Ardnamurchan in the far west – near Polloch, to be more precise. He didn't have the comforts of home at the old schoolhouse awaiting him when the day was over – instead he had to stay in a crude workmen's hostel somewhere in the empty hills. His journey to Polloch itself was nightmarish enough with the faulty wiring in the Pride of the Glen leaving him navigating the latter part of the run by moonlight along strange and dangerous narrow roads. He managed to make it safely and began his stint on the dizzy twists and gradients with all the other various contractors who had their vehicles working on this project. One day (he told me during our recent conversation) he had stopped the ERF on a steep incline and had stepped down to relieve himself by the roadside. "Pride of the Glen" had a crude handbrake system that had to be ratcheted up for it to grip and hold and he had delivered the requisite number of pulls on the lever. He left the engine running though and the heavy vibrations had slowly disengaged the ratchet. He looked up to see the immense bulk of the fully loaded Pride of the Glen gathering momentum as it began to make its dash for freedom. And it got worse. Another lorry was labouring its way up the steep hill, also fully loaded, and was directly in its path. The driver leaped from his cab a moment before impact – in the nick of time as the pitiless bulk of the ERF tossed it contemptuously aside and left it badly damaged and lying ignominiously in the heather at the side of the road. As I was noting down these details, I asked my brother, for no particular reason, what kind of lorry had been the one knocked out of the game.

"It was a Bedford OB; one of Pat the Pier's", he said.

I paused. Surely not?

"What colour was it?"

"A sort of acid green," was the reply. "It was a bit of a wreck even before I hit it."

Yes, it was the very same lorry that had almost done for me just a few weeks earlier when it had reared up like some steed pawing the air. It had just been sent out on another job after I had had my replacement Morris diesel. Such were the conditions that prevailed in the almost unregulated days of the late nineteen fifties.

There is a still more unlikely footnote to all this.   Instead of being left to moulder away into dust on a remote Highland mountainside, it was rescued by its driver and taken back to some yard or garage premises where he managed to get it repaired sufficiently to return to the Polloch road project.   Its thin desperate engine note was a familiar one to my brother for the rest of his spell on that job.

Jeep

Yet another of the highly eccentric vehicles that still stands out in my memory from those days is a very battered and rickety former military jeep. It was the real McCoy and may even have played some heroic role in the D Day landings for all I know. I first saw it standing forlornly in a courtyard during my brief spell of employment as ghillie/ponyman by the Glenmoriston Estates. For some reason I have now completely forgotten, I had been sent to help out in my ponyman capacity on the Cullachy Estate at the north end of the Corriearrick Pass several miles to the west of Fort Augustus village. Clearly, this estate must have come under the control of the eccentric Captain Hunt of Invergarry Hotel, about whom I have already spoken. Before getting to the subject of the jeep and how it nearly killed me twice on the same day, a word about the gamekeeper who worked then on the Cullachy Estate. He was a young local man from Fort Augustus called Lea MacNally. In later years, Lea was to become one of Scotland's most outstanding naturalists and photographers of Highland wild life. He was to publish several books and to become a highly articulate expert on that subject on many radio and television programmes. Before his untimely death in 1993, he had been a Ranger in Torridon and had been made a Fellow of the Royal Zoological Society. The Lea MacNally I knew in those earlier days I am now talking about was a small, intense, dark man, designed by nature to wear tweed and deerstalker hats and to have a stalker's telescope hanging from his shoulder. (Actually, I did occasionally meet him in what could almost be called social occasions in the village hall when he took part in the badminton club evenings with a silent ruthlessness that destroyed all opposition.) On the estate, he was a man of very few words. He said no more to me than was necessary to indicate my duties. The job was much the same as on the Glenmoriston hills. I was the anonymous, invisible presence who guided the pony that carried the dead stag off the hill after the wealthy guest had killed it with his or her rifle under the expert guidance of the gamekeeper. And few there must have been in the Highlands who could have matched Lea MacNally for those skills.

Anyway, to return to the Jeep. I saw it sitting in the yard on the very first morning of that brief stint in Cullachy. It looked as if it had just emerged from the Battle of the Bulge. It was battered, scuffed and green/khaki-coloured. It had lumpy, knotted tyres for churning over rugged terrain and just seemed to be crying out to be pointed at the nearest narrow track into the hills and let loose. But it was not for me. My short stay at Cullachy was unremarkable mainly in that the distances I had to cover each day were much shorter than in the Glenmoriston hills – and also I was much nearer my home at Fort Augustus. Then one day, Lea broke the silence of the hills that he usually had wrapped around him and told me that I was to drive the Jeep to Grant's Garage in the village to get some service or other done on it. This was my chance. I had a brief practice spin on it and soon became aware of the very special qualities of this amazing little creation. It was permanently fixed in four-wheel-drive mode and this alone was quite startling to experience for the first time. But the main delight for me was the gearbox. One of the biggest problems of driving in the Fifties was getting down into first gear while the vehicle was in motion. The double-de-clutch method was the only way and this demanded subtlety and skill. To mis-time it could cause a shriek of tormented metal and a very red face. Not with the marvellous Jeep. It had, as I recollect, a three-speed gearbox and it had the silky delights of synchromesh all the way through. In spite of the Cullachy Jeep being pretty old it was as nippy and responsive as ever you could have wished for in those days of normally sluggish commercial vehicles.

Now, to give you the full background to the story of what was lying in wait for me very soon now, I will have to re-introduce Hector. I have spoken about him earlier in these pages, but to summarise once more: he was the son of the local Free Church minister, Reverend MacLeod. Everything about Reverend MacLeod that told of his severe faith in terms of austere presence and views on human frailty were to be found in his son in the exact opposite form. What I am trying to say – with almost forensic tact – is that Hector was not the ideal son of the manse. For some reason that completely escapes me now, Hector was with me at Cullachy that day. Had he a student job there like me – he was then attending Aberdeen University like myself - or had he just tagged along with me that day? I have no idea. What I can say is that when it came to the basic skills of picking up the best-looking girls in his immediate neighbourhood, Hector was the envy of all of us. But in the matter of taking control of awkward vehicles – well, I considered that that was my territory.

My tackety boots clattered on the all-metal floor of the Jeep as I clambered into the crude, canvas-backed driver's seat (the only seat) and then the engine burst into a satisfying roar. Hector had climbed in behind and we were off down the narrow, tree-lined road towards Ardachy, heading eventually for the Glendoe road where it ran along the west shore of Loch Ness. But Hector was getting to be a bit of a pest. He wanted to have a shot of the Jeep. However, by now I was coming to terms with some of its finer points: its four wheel drive; its almost non-existent brakes and, worst of all, its slack and almost anarchic steering. Each bump or pothole sent the front wheels on their own individual quests for freedom. Constant correction by the steering wheel on its long, thin column was essential just to keep us on the road. Such a deadly projectile being let loose on a public road today would be laughable – but the Fifties were a more tolerant era. Hector was getting more and more insistent. Eventually I gave in. "All right. You can have a shot."

I pulled up just at the bridge at Ardachy.

"You can take it to the Tarff bridge and that's all. I'll have to take it the rest of the way – through the village."

I gave some instruction on how to handle the wayward steering then I clambered into the back, more than a little nervous as Hector engaged the clutch and hurled us on our way again. My fears were all too swiftly realised. Hector was clearly enjoying himself in control of the powerful and still-lively engine under the flat bonnet but he was rapidly losing control. We were soon swaying sickeningly from side to side of the narrow road and all the while I was remembering the frightening ditch on the right hand side a few hundred yards up ahead. It was deep, dark and menacing.

"It's all right," Hector yelled back at me over his shoulder. "I've got the hang of it now."

The right front wheel struck the verge and immediately plunged into the black peaty depths. A large willow tree clutched at us like an arrester hook and the Jeep slammed to a violent stop. It flung its rear end up into the air – the bit of the Jeep I was desperately clinging to – and I was flung forward into the barbed wire embrace of the willow tree.

Silence. At first I could not see Hector. I was a mass of scratches but nothing was broken. Then a groan from nearby told me that my driver had survived as well. Hector heaved himself from behind the steering wheel of the trapped Jeep. He was in a similar mess to me. By now I had found out that the main casualty was my army khaki battledress trousers. The left leg had been neatly torn off, right up at the hip and was now flopped down over my ankle. I presented a clownish and very undignified sight. I was in too much a state of shock to let loose with some expletives in Hector's direction. The immediate problem was what to do next. We climbed over a fence and stumbled across a field and found ourselves approaching the back door of the Kirks' farmhouse. Mrs Kirk came to the door and after first recoiling in some alarm at the dazed and ragged figures on her doorstep, she called for her husband. He got his tractor out of its shed and she got safety pins. The tractor easily hauled the stricken Jeep back on to the road while Mrs Kirk used the pins to restore some dignity to my collapsed trouser leg.

The Jeep's amazing engine roared into immediate life when the starter was pressed and after thanking our rescuer, we resumed our journey – extremely cautiously now and with me at the wheel. I suppose I can, by way of an excuse, say that I was still in a state of shock. This could account for the fact that soon after we had joined the road that led to the village, I began to press down on the accelerator again – just to feel for one last time the marvellous response from the engine just in front of me. The speed increased until we were fairly scudding along as if we hadn't a care and nothing whatever had happened. But something had happened: something we could never have imagined. The bonnet of a Jeep hinged upwards from just under the windscreen and the clamps to secure it were at the front. When we had slammed into that ditch these clamps had been loosened, so that when our speed had reached a critical point, the bonnet suddenly reared up, slamming violently against the windscreen. It in turn partially collapsed against the steering wheel, trapping my hand in the process. And yes, it was extremely painful. So I was now in pain, blinded and bewildered. What, in God's name, next? Luckily, instinct had me stand up to see where we were heading so that we were able to avoid another off-road experience. I pulled up fiercely, realising that this Jeep was just not for me. Get it to Grant's garage before it finally got me.

And that was the last time I ever saw it. Shortly afterwards I was recalled to the vast open spaces of the hills of Glenmoriston with nothing more frightening there than the flatulence of the big black horse I was in charge of.

Son of Albion

I spent two memorable summers in the late fifties at Laggan Bridge. This tiny village is about eight miles to the west of Newtonmore on the Spean Bridge road. In those days, my uncle, David Miller and my Aunt Annie owned the village general store. This shop was the hub of the scattered community and provided all the basic provisions for a huge swathe of the surrounding Highland countryside.

My Uncle Dave had asked me to help out that summer and drive his travelling shop on all of the four different weekly routes he covered. Each of these runs had its own character arising from the driving problems of the actual stretches of road as well as the variety of the customers who lived on these routes. Fascinating as each of those runs was, the most outstanding memory of that first Laggan working holiday is of the quite incredible vehicle that I was placed in charge of and which I navigated along those roads throughout that unforgettable summer.

My uncle was still using a 1930s (I can't remember the precise date) Albion van: registration number BSP 472. It was of a style known in its day as a "Bread Van". How to convey its sheer massiveness?

I suppose it would look rather insignificant if standing alongside a behemoth of today's motorways but in my memory it looms immense. It was square and upright and had not the tiniest concession to streamlining. It's almost as if its grim, Calvinistic Scottish designers set out to defy the aerodynamic lines that were becoming popular in the thirties, seeing them as the designs of the devil. It had a long bonnet with a vast radiator at the end that looked like an ancient classical Greek temple. On the top of this radiator was a small temperature gauge which the driver could use as a sort of gun-sight to aim the huge projectile along the narrow twisting roads of Badenoch and Glenshiro.

But it was inside the Spartan wooden cab that the real drama was to unfold. It was here that you came face up with machinery at its most basic and malevolent. The Albion was indeed a monster. It had to be treated like no other vehicle I had driven up till then – or like any other since. You could never relax on the assumption that you had it sussed out. The only way to convey this sense of teetering on the edge of hysteria when driving the Albion will have to be a blow-by-blow account of my very first encounter with it. However, first of all I have to put my driving skills into perspective. It truth be told, I was more than a little bit cocky. Back in those days, all vehicles were much more individualistic than they are today. But, I had been around and had driven many different types so that I felt that I had about seen it all. The long-forgotten skill of double-de-clutching (essential in the days before modern silky synchronised gearboxes) was a dawdle to me. I thought, in short, that I could drive anything – anywhere. On that first dreadful morning, Uncle Dave was to accompany me to Newtonmore railway station to pick up the bread from the Perth bakeries to be taken back to Laggan.

"I'll take it for the first bit," he announced.

I watched him climb up to and over the huge handbrake that blocked access to the driver's side of the cabin when it was pulled on. It looked as solid and heavy as the lever in a railway signal box.

"Now, watch. First of all, the pedals are different."

"Different. How are they different?"

And he told me. Indeed they were different. The order from left to right was: clutch, accelerator and footbrake.

Yes, you've spotted it. The accelerator was in the middle. But that was as nothing when compared to the gearbox. I came to think of it as not only alive but as being filled with hate and permanently just about to tip over into madness. You have never heard a sound like the flaying of metal when an Albion gear-shift has gone astray by so much as a nanosecond. The agony is transmitted up the steel gear lever to set the very bone-marrow curdling.

Things actually began quite casually that morning. Uncle Dave drove calmly along past Gaskmore reminding me that double-de-clutching was essential. Yes, yes. I knew all that. But it was the additional startling detail that you had to double-de-clutch while changing UP through the gears as well as down that brought the first sense of unease. Ye gods. Then there were the brakes. They were utterly primitive. They were rod and cable operated so you had to have keen anticipation if you expected to stop anywhere in the general area you intended. As for emergencies – well, you were not meant to have any of them.

It was now time to change places with Uncle Dave and take over the controls. And it was now that the problems began. I found out immediately that I could not change up from first gear to second. I did all that I had seen my uncle do and all that he had told me – and more – but the shuddering gear lever simply refused to force obedience from the churning hell below the floorboards. I found out pretty early on that if you missed a gear change on the Albion, there was only one thing you could do. You had to pull up and start all over again from scratch. After a spell of this misery there was nothing for it but to ask my uncle to take over again. I was silent and completely crushed. He drove a mile or two, flipping up and down the gearbox and then suggested that I should have another go. I fought again with that hellish gear lever in a state of total and utter disbelief that all my driving skills should have abandoned me. It was after another period of sending the shriek of tortured gears echoing over the strath that it happened. Suddenly and for no apparent reason, the Albion relented and allowed me just a hint of co-operation. I built nervously on this and by the time we were heading back to Laggan Bridge again, I actually thought that I was getting the hang of it. But I was to learn that you could never make such a rash assumption and that you ever were master of the Albion. Throughout all of that marvellous summer the threat of disaster was ever present. Each morning as I braced myself in front of the towering radiator, clasping the brass grip on the starting handle, I would begin a feverish rehearsal in my mind of all the things that might lie out there in store for me that day. Even the act of starting the Albion up could lay you low if you mistimed the heavy swing and the handle kicked back after you had goaded the ancient engine into reluctant life.

On the road back from Glenshiro there used to be a small ford that you had to cross. I was warned by Uncle Dave of the special dangers of this. Water would affect the brakes: changing their normal uselessness into absolute total uselessness. A few hundred yards further on from this ford there was a steep brae leading down to a narrow bridge. Immediately on the other side of that bridge was a sharp 90-degree right turn. To avoid serious trouble I was told that immediately the van had heaved itself out of the water, I was to keep depressing the brake pedal and hauling on the hand-brake to help to dry out the primitive brake pads. On one of my early runs on that road, I had forgotten to take these precautions until too late. I had found myself in the middle of a daytime nightmare – literally falling down this violently steep hill, encased in the dead-weight tonnage of the Albion with its tumbling cargo of groceries; both feet braced on the shuddering footbrake while simultaneously hauling back the monstrous hand-brake lever. Gradually the brakes began to bite and slowed my plunge just in time. This was a mistake you only made the once.

I really did enjoy that long-ago summer holiday job and the daily challenge thrown down by the Albion. I think one of the reasons was the fact that while you were in charge (partially, anyway) of that monster, you had the enormous satisfaction of knowing for an absolute certainty that nobody else on the road, anywhere, at that moment could have climbed into the Albion's cab and coaxed even the tiniest scrap of co-operation out of it.

One of the most enjoyable of the several runs that Miller's Grocery van undertook in the week was the one to Ardverickie House on the shores of Loch Laggan. The world knows this amazing building nowadays as television's Glenbogle House from the somewhat loose (to put it mildly) adaptations of Compton Mackenzie's "Monarch of the Glen". In those days, it was the enormous fairy-tale house-cum-castle that lay at the end of a long stretch of private road that began with a narrow bridge and a castellated gate-house just off the Spean Bridge/Laggan road. The estate in those days was owned by a wealthy family that even had members of the royal family as guests staying with them in the summer. More about that shortly. There were quite a number of houses to call at in the estate and we (myself and my young cousin, Jim) always stopped at the very first one for our lunch. The same routine each time of picking something from the shelves in the van and having the wife of the house making some tea for us to accompany it. After that, there was the drive through the most amazing scenery, calling in at various stops and eventually arriving at Ardverickie House itself. We always had a large order to deliver there and would take the Albion round to the back to the kitchen entrance. I remember this kitchen as being dark and high ceilinged with shelves and with pots and other kitchen implements hanging all around. On more than one occasion, I managed to venture into the main part of the house and stare at the dark-panelled walls with the rows of antlered heads and vast portraits in the main hall, with the impressive, sweeping staircase leading to the mysteries of the upper floors.

I mentioned the visits from royalty at Ardverickie House. On one occasion my poor uncle was to make a bit of a fool of himself. It was around lunch time on a Sunday. The newspapers were sold from the shop and were stacked up in the front lobby. I had been sitting beside the window and noticed a Land Rover drawing up at the petrol pump at the other side of the road. I mentioned it to my uncle and he glanced out.

"It's Lady Fielden", he muttered. He looked again. "And she's got the princes with her."

These were the Princes of Gloucester - and I have forgotten who the other one was -who were just youths then. Two lanky figures in shabby jackets and the inevitable Wellington boots of the aristocracy. No need to describe the titled lady in the tweed uniform of her class. My uncle was galvanised and began to rush to get to the pump and see to the filling up of the Land Rover. He had just got in from church, and like most church elders in these days, had been wearing the traditional navy-blue suit. On the way out, through the kitchen door, he reached up and grabbed the jacket hanging at the back, and began to shrug himself into it. I watched him as he emerged from the front door, heading towards the group standing at the pump. He looked very strange and appeared to be in some difficulty - as if he could not get into his jacket properly. I then saw what the problem was. As a student in Aberdeen in those days, I possessed the appropriate uniform – the dark navy blazer with the supernova gold-red-yellow (and other colours too) badge on the breast pocket. Also I was quite slight of stature. Much more so than Uncle Dave. And it was my blazer that he had grabbed from the back of the door on his headlong dash outside to the VIP customers. By the time he had reached the pump, the blazer had been forced on and he looked grotesque with his high hunched shoulders and restricted movements. The incongruous badge completed the hilarious sight. We watched him as he struggled with the pump handle and laughed cruelly as he stumbled back into the house with scarlet-faced embarrassment.

The following summer, I was back in Laggan Bridge for another spell as driver of the Miller Stores travelling shop. Same job – but this time without the Albion. It had gone. In its place was the latest BMC product of the ill-fated factory at Bathgate.
It was luxury. Harrods on wheels. I won't pretend that I missed the vicious old brute with its primitive amenities and daemonic unpredictability. Nevertheless, as I swept nonchalantly up the narrow track to another remote, shepherd's house, I knew full well that all the relaxed skills I now had at the wheel of a large commercial vehicle came directly from the harsh training grounds I had been on the previous year. I owed it all to the old dun-coloured Albion with its profound instinctive hatred for the whole human race.

Bob Miller's Mill

One Easter, when I was sixteen years old, I thought I'd have a change in my holiday job. I'd go for something different. Most holiday jobs up till then it had normally been the good old Forestry Commission. Now was the time to strike out and do something a bit more adventurous. Also a chance to make a bit more money.

I had heard that there was a sawmill that had started up at Auchterawe, to the west of the village and it was on the lookout for an assistant. The mill was away at the very end of the dark, narrow Forestry road – and then a bit further. Away up beyond the nurseries for the infant trees; well past the impressive Forester's house where the slightly aristocratic Drummonds resided; even beyond the very last house in Auchterawe where the MacDonald family lived. It was right at the foot of a sudden surge of hill which we were told in those days was the site of an ancient vitrified fort. For all that intriguing tale, it is strange that I never actually went up to find out for myself. Here it was that Bob Miller had set up his sawmill.

Bob Miller was from the North East: from the mysterious lands beyond Nairn and Forres where the people spoke in strange tongues and accents. He was probably in his early fifties and had a vast reservoir of seething energy on tap. I found myself engaged immediately with instructions to be at the mill at eight o'clock the following morning. Sharp. I was left with no doubt that sharp meant just that.

It was then - even before I actually began this new job – that it was dawning on me that I was about to enter a very different world of employment from the one to which I had become accustomed up till then. I refer to the dear old Forestry Commission. The Commission didn't drive you too hard in those days. There was a sort of unwritten code that laid down just how fast any job ought to be done and that code tended to err on the side of the kindly and humane. (I have already dealt with this theme elsewhere.) Rests could not be taken too blatantly, though. When it rained you got under cover fast, safe in the knowledge that your pay wasn't being docked.

Now I found that I was stuck with Bob Miller for the whole long, agonising working day. Not the remotest chance of relaxing or taking the occasional fly break in the time-honoured Forestry style. My new master's daily routine was an endless, remorseless heaving of logs and guiding them up to and through the shredding teeth of the blurred circular saw that dominated everything in that clearing – both in the unnerving shrillness of its note and in its voracious demand for more and more timber to rip through. His day had usually begun long before I made my own appearance at eight o'clock. As I was still pedalling my way up the winding Auchterawe road, from miles away I could hear the thudding of the engine of the big Fordson tractor that drove the saw, with the accompanying rise and fall of the scream of the circular blade. The actual starting up of that mighty engine every morning was quite a performance, which I witnessed on one or two occasions. Memory is such a fragile thing and all of this took place a very, very long time ago, but this is what I think happened. The tractor had two fuels: petrol and paraffin. The latter was called TVO, or Tractor Vaporising Oil. First, a tap was turned on from the small petrol tank and after all manner of ritual priming of carburettor and choke and things, Bob Miller would brace himself against the huge radiator, grasp the starting handle and begin to haul it round. The wheezings and gulpings would eventually – after massive efforts – explode into violent life and the engine would send its thunder bouncing off the hills around. He would leave it to run for a spell and when he reckoned the engine was sufficiently hot, the petrol was turned off and the main fuel, the TVO, was now fed in. This it was that kept the show on the road for the rest of the long, long day.

I always felt a sort of curious pride when I told people who asked about my sawmill job. "The engine runs on paraffin. No kidding." It always had a quirky feel about it.

I had three main jobs at the saw-mill. The first was to stack the squared-off timber props that were the main product of the mill. The logs were steered through the circular saw by being pushed manually along a bench of rollers. The miller would heave up the log, align it, and then, slowly and carefully, guide it forward. All the time listening to the sound of the blade; never letting the banshee shriek fall below a certain level. The ever-present dangers were, either stalling the engine and jamming the blade or at the very worst, having the blade disintegrate. So he told me anyway, and I wasn't in any position to argue with him. The log would go through at least four times, each time having a slice shaved off the outside. Result: a perfectly squared-off beam of white timber. The strips that were shaved off were thrown aside - called slabs, or backs. I had to carry the finished trimmed props away and stack them. This was done carefully. First of all, two were placed parallel, then the next two at right angles across them leaving a hollow square, and so on up till the stack was about my own height. Not too demanding work if done at a steady pace, as the props weren't too heavy and as they were squared off, were easy enough to fit into place. If it was the only job, it would have kept me on the move steadily all day: tiring, but manageable. Life wasn't permitted to be that easy under the rule of Bob Miller. There were the backs to be dragged to their dump as well. This was a real spirit-crusher. There seemed to be so many of them - far out of proportion to the number of props that were processed. They flew from the blade, whipping out alongside the bench - long, floppy and oozing with resin. This resin soaked into the clothing, the pores and probably into the very bone marrow. If this was your life's job, it would seep into the depths of your soul as well. Maybe this accounted for Bob Miller's occasional outbursts. Sometimes the backs would accumulate so much that they threatened to hold up the work. This was the most unforgivable sin in the saw miller's catechism. I might be heading off to the prop stack with more beams, when the Buchan accents would part even the scream of the saw: "Gie's a bit mair effort, laddie; whit the hell's wrang wi' ye ...?" and I'd have to rush to clear the latest pile of these ragged abominations.

Finally, there was the third task. This was the regular emptying of the sawdust pit under the blade. You don't need to have too much imagination to realise that this also would need someone who did this job and no other. Think of the torrents of sawdust that streamed from the blade in a normal day. Not dust really, but large flakes of pale timber. Now, obviously the blade would have to stop to let someone get underneath to shovel this stuff out. Just as obviously, when the blade wasn't spinning, the work of the mill was held up. A torment for Bob Miller, which he resolved in typical no-nonsense manner. Admittedly, he would occasionally shut off the mighty Fordson for a complete clear out of the pit, and I would shovel the light insubstantial stuff out as fast as possible (remember, it couldn't be left lying there, and would have to be carried off to another separate dump in a wheelbarrow later). However, there were other times when I had to scoop it out while the blade was still running. The pit was deep, and I was never actually all that near the blade, but it was pretty scary all the same.

Perhaps the strongest image I have from those days of half a century ago is of Bob Miller's left hand. I would occasionally watch him as he shoved a log into the blade. The tip of the saw would emerge sometimes and other times would be buried deep in it, depending on how thick the timber was. He would leave his left hand on the log, right up till the last second before shifting it back to safety. What chilled the imagination was that his left hand had lost its last three fingers in a long-ago accident leaving just index and thumb, and he would let that blade sometimes move so close that it was actually spinning where those fingers used to be. It wasn't bravado - it just didn't bother him.

I still have a memento of that long-ago Easter holiday job. It's called an Altair "Incabloc" and it's a wristwatch. In Inverness, in those days, there was a small jewellers' shop on Church Street called Kelly's. My father had told me that it was sometimes possible to buy bankruptcy stock there. Well I was lucky, and from the window stacked with decanters and crystal glasses, I picked out the watch that was to last me literally the rest of my life. I only use it now while working in the garden, and it is scratched and battered looking, but the old red second hand still sweeps its way round the scarred face in sort of reasonable accuracy. The only tangible relic of Bob Miller and his ferocious work-ethic.

Perkeo 1

This account of long-ago employment in Glenmoriston was prompted by a delving into a box file where I have been stuffing instruction manuals for all the gadgets and devices that have accrued to me over the decades. A recent excavation into the deeper geological strata revealed a still-smart little booklet with "Voigtländer PERKEO I. Instructions for Use". The illustration on the cover shows a rugged-looking bellows camera, extended and ready for taking pictures.

Much more than the memory of a wonderful old camera flows back when I look at this instruction manual. How I originally came to own it and its attendant collection of gadgets is a story in its own right.

I had had a spell working on the construction of one of the roads that went far up into the hills in Glenmoriston – either for the Forestry Commission or for the Hydro Electric schemes. On this job, I had no lorry or jeep to drive but had only a selection of shovels and forks (graips) for spreading the loads of gravel and sand that were tipped out to provide a surface for the basic kind of road being built. Now, at this point, I have no idea as to who was my employer. I do know that there were many others working on this particular project and occasionally I got to know some of them quite well. For some reason, there were not many of the usual gang from the village. The greater bulk of each 12 hour working day (seven in the morning till seven at night) was spent in the company of a fellow spreader of gravel who was the son of a well-known lay preacher. We were two tiny figures on the vastness of the empty hillside at the very tip of the ribbon of crudely surfaced road and it was on the whole, a pretty depressing experience. My companion was not malevolent or in any way ill-disposed to me – it's just that he was about the most primitive life-form I have ever been forced to spend time with. Conversation was minimal and was as basic as you can imagine. It was dominated by the staccato "f" word, which could be used as the four basic parts of speech: noun, verb, adverb and adjective. Now, I used this word myself as it was a part of the normal linguistic currency in the work squads in those days as well, but in this concentration it was a desperately depressing thing to have to listen to. After we had attacked the last load to be tipped out and spread it over the roughly gouged-out by bulldozers foundation, there would be little or no conversation except for the occasional crackle of oaths. I remember sitting down in the heather looking far down into the glen to pick out the first sign of the next load as it began to grind its way up towards us and hoping that my companion just kept his mouth shut.

But, to get back to the camera. One of my fellow road squad workers lived in a rough looking caravan parked near the main road that ran through the glen. He was an amiable sort and we got on well together. This was not all that often, but when our paths did cross, we would have a bit of banter. Then one day he told me that he had been falling foul of "The Pole", (explanation clearly not necessary) the notoriously choleric foreman who was the overseer of this particular part of the job and that his future was looking far from secure. Actually I witnessed the episode that caused the final flare-up. A vast concrete mixer had been required to be shifted to another site further down the hill and The Pole had ordered it to be attached by its solid metal towing bar to the back of a lorry. This concrete mixer was a really frightening contraption and totally unsuited to the kind of terrain on which it was being used. It was very tall; it had unshod, iron wheels and had a very narrow wheel-base so that even standing on a level surface it looked unstable. When it began to move over a rough, unmetalled road surface, pitted with holes and undulations, it would always be teetering on the edge of disaster. The Pole had organised us into two teams – one on either side of the mixer. Then he instructed us to fasten ropes to the top of the cement mixer and to move alongside it while it was being towed. We were ordered to pit our puny combined weights against the massive tonnage of the mixer should it threaten to topple over on its side. We all felt uneasy about this arrangement. My pal from the caravan began to argue with the foreman and voices were raised. The Pole insisted that it was perfectly a feasible plan while his opponent said that there was not the faintest chance that five or six of us on either side of the vast mixer could do anything to stop it from falling over if it decided to do so. The Pole, being the foreman, won the argument. The lorry driver engaged the clutch and the crazy pantomime procession set off. The six of us on either side of the dangerously swaying mass of dull, dead-weight metal strained dutifully on our ropes. Hardly had a few yards been covered when the wheels on one side started to sink. The six on the other side immediately felt the huge weight on their ropes and just as immediately realised that there was no future in attempting to hang on. The monstrous tower of metal was now leaning over the team on the lee side – that included me – and we fled as it crashed into the heather. An image I still have fixed in my memory is of the solid iron tow-bar, which twisted like a stick of liquorice with the forces that had been brought to bear on it. This was not a good moment for my pal to choose to address the now-apoplectic Pole along the lines of "I told you so..." His dismissal was as swift and closed to debate or discussion as one would expect in those days. Later on, I called by at the caravan to find my pal (his name I have long ago forgotten) packing up his possessions. He was not in the best of form and unloaded his feelings about how he had been treated. Nothing surprising there. Then it was that he drew my attention to his amazing camera. It had a gleaming brown leather case and the neck-strap had four small leather cases with either studs or zips on them that contained the various gadgets that went with it. They included a metal lens hood, a small flash unit, a light meter and a thing called a "Kontur Finder". This latter slid into the shoe on top of the camera and saved you having to squint into the tiny viewfinder that all cameras had in those days. You just looked through the Kontur with your right eye, keeping the left eye open, and you could see the superimposition of the frame of the picture in white as you looked at the scene. It was actually an excellent idea.

"I'm really short of cash," he told me. "Any chance you'd like to buy it?"

Did I want to buy it!

Everything in my entire being groaned for it – but with a hopeless longing. It was clearly beyond my pathetic resources.

"How much would you want for it?"

"I couldn't go anything below twenty pounds," was the answer.

In those days that was one hefty sum of money. Then I had a blaze of inspiration.

"How about this?" I said. "Instead of heading straight back to Inverness, how about turning west at Invermoriston and going to Fort Augustus. It's only six miles. My father's headmaster of the school there. I'll give you directions and a note you can hand to him. It should be all right."

This was a pretty long shot. The note went along the lines of,

"Dad.

*This is genuine. I want to buy this camera. You pay the bearer £20
and I'll pay you back later.*
Thanks."

It would take me quite a while to pay this money back but to me it
was more than worth it.

The rest of that interminable day on the hill – the afternoon of it spent
in the monosyllabic company of my usual companion – was absolute
purgatory. I had no way of knowing if my father would have paid
the £20 to a total stranger or just told him to clear off. When I did
eventually get back to the old schoolhouse in Fort Augustus some
time after eight o'clock, my nerves were taut and I could scarcely
contain myself. I knew that it had been a very bold initiative on my
part. I knew my father well enough to understand that he didn't dole
out money in a casual fashion. Or maybe it was that I had calculated
that he and I shared one trait – or character failing – in life. A love of
gadgets. And the Perkeo I Voigtlander kit was truly a magnificent
collection of gadgets.

But it paid off. I approached the back door with deepest trepidation
and opened it. And there it was, in all its glory, lying on the kitchen
table. Not only were there the little leather pouches for the various
gadgets, there was an additional bag with the instruction manuals and
a set of coloured lens filters as well. My cup of happiness indeed
was running over. I had accurately gauged that my father would have
been seduced by the sight of the Voigtlander. I can't remember how
long it took me to pay him back the nineteen fifties, mind-blowing
sum of twenty pounds, but pay it back I did. There were no
concessions from my father on this matter.

Compared to today's almost exclusively automatic cameras, the
Perkeo I was an unbelievably cumbersome thing to use. The
maximum number of photos on each roll of film was eight. Before
you could get around to releasing the shutter you had to take a
reading on the light meter and adjust the aperture accordingly. Next
came the distance meter measuring and the appropriate lens
adjustment. Now line up the frame of the intended picture in the
"Kontur Finder" before depressing the release with its curiously
modest ping sound. But the main thing was the photographs that this
camera took. Even though it is almost fifty years since I last used it,
the modest number I actually did take – especially the colour
transparency ones on Agfa film - are still among the best I have ever

taken.   If only I had taken more, I feel, what a marvellous record I would have had. But the simple truth is that the film and the processing were too damned expensive in those days.

Little Did We Know

And now – one last motoring tale to round things off. It is sparked off by the discovery of a long-lost photo.

The photograph itself is innocent enough. It shows an elderly lady in a flowery print frock and dated cloche hat. Beside her stands a smartly suited woman who is holding her arm and with her other hand is gripping a large, black handbag. The smartly-suited woman is my mother and the other is my grandmother. They are both standing in front of a slightly rakish-looking red car with chrome stripe along the side and a black fabric roof. It is the 1949 Riley one and a half litre saloon, and I was just about to take my mother and my grandmother (my mother's mother) for a run up Glengarry. The year was 1958 and I was at home from Aberdeen University during the summer holiday. I don't remember what holiday job I was doing on this occasion to earn my vital cash for survival as a student, but clearly this photo must have been taken on a Sunday. On all the other days there would not have been time for such trivia as going for runs in the car. And, yes, the photograph itself. It is in colour – a rare thing from the universally grey fifties. I had recently bought my Kodak "Colorsnap" camera, a reasonably-priced introduction to colour photography that was being promoted in those days to make that luxury available for the less affluent. It used a curious size of film that was slightly larger than the soon-to-be-universal 35mm. But the results were startlingly good and provided a welcome change in my records from the universal dullness of the bulk of my fifties pictures. (The Voigtlander camera didn't appear till later on.) The photo was taken beside the "Back Place", as we called it – the wooden appendage to the traditional 19th century schoolhouse that was our home in those days. It contained the coke-fired stove, the electric cooker and our space for normal daily meals. My mother was ever decrying its graceless appearance and rudimentary amenities. But it was snug enough in the winter months when the Rayburn was thrumming with heat. The Riley was the pride and joy of the old schoolhouse, even although my father rarely drove it himself. It was something that we never really managed to figure out, but my father always made a point of owning high-profile cars. Again, I have spoken about this before, but to recap - in his own youthful pre-war days, it was the MG sports car that defined his motoring. During the war, again as I have mentioned elsewhere, it was his largely-unused Triumph Gloria. Then in the early fifties came the disastrous 1939 SS Jaguar. This was followed by the beautiful Riley here and it, in turn, made way not long after for the unbelievable luxury of the 3.4 litre automatic transmission Jaguar, NST 39. (I still see that number plate around the town and cannot but feel that it ought to be mine! Ron, at the garage where my father had sold it, persuaded me that it was just too much trouble to buy a number plate back then in the seventies.) But he was not a keen driver and always saw to it that either my brother or I would do the actual piloting of the Denoon vehicle whenever a journey was to be made. No problem as far as we were concerned as we were both ever eager to oblige. When he did drive, it was with a sort of nervous reluctance. This was more than likely the consequence of my mother being one of the worst passengers in the world. Only with him, I have to add here. My brother and I could get by with only minimal dark mutterings about speed or closeness to vehicles ahead. But when it was my father behind the wheel, a journey of any length was accompanied by a low relentless threnody of mutterings of the phrase, "Oh Dear"; "Oh Dear"; "Oh Dear!" then intensifying into "Oh Dear Dear"; "Oh Dear Dear" "Oh Dear Dear". This would expand further into something like, "You're going too fast into this corner, Robert. You're going too fast!" The ultimate morale crusher for my wretched father was the occasion when she announced, with a sharp finality: "Just stop the car, Robert. I'm going to get out and walk the rest of the way home from here." This was somewhere along the Lochside between Drumnadrochit and Invermoriston. We would sit and watch the whitening of his knuckles on the steering wheel during these awful journeys but had to admire the restraint he showed in not erupting in wrath. It was all being tamped down, though, and was responsible for him all but giving up driving for a long spell of his life after my brother and I had passed our driving tests.

But to get back to the photograph. I only recently came across it and had been impressed with how close it brought me to that day. It also brought a jolt of a more unpleasant kind: the jolt of a thoroughly unpleasant memory. All looks so innocent in the pose of the two subjects. The weather looks good and the Riley provided a stylish and comfortable mode of travel on the roads of those days. But we little know what lurks out there on the twisting Highland roads to bring our little world crashing down on us. The first part of the day went by without too much drama. The run up Glengarry in those days was more of an adventure in the fifties for two main reasons. First was the actual road itself. It was narrow, winding and rose and fell like a plunging switchback. The wits had to be well and truly at peak sharpness just to navigate it. But there was also the heavy traffic caused by the Hydro Electric schemes – frequent thundering lorries and buses with workmen either heading to their fierce tasks or returning to their camps. As I have described elsewhere, there was a huge workers' camp at Invergarry where I had had a summer job myself. But, as I have suggested, the run itself was pleasing but unremarkable – until we were about five or six miles from the village of Invergarry, on the way home. Without warning, the magnificent Riley, which had done all that was asked of it with its normal élan, suddenly became an inert mass of useless metal and glass. The clutch failed. It just remained flat to the floor and did nothing. A slack and useless metal appendage. I rolled into a lay-by and contemplated the situation. Already, the seriousness of it had begun to settle on me. The passengers too both became alarmed – my mother in particular. She, you will recollect, was notorious in the family for her deep pessimism as to the safety – even the basic wisdom - of road travel. My grandmother was more philosophical as I seem to remember. At first, it looked as if all we had to do was to wait for some passing vehicle to be flagged down. There would be little problem in begging a lift with the passengers I was carrying. But the perversity of life that day seemed to be arranging it that what few desultory vehicles were still on that road, were going in the wrong direction. So it was that we decided that the next thing was to get in touch with my father to let him know that there had been a breakdown. Then I'd have to phone Grant's garage in Fort Augustus to get a mechanic out to help or more likely to arrange to get the car towed back to the village. It was now late afternoon and we would by now have been expected to have ground our way up Bunoich Brae and into the playground at the back of the old schoolhouse well before tea-time. No chance of that now. I noticed there was a modest-looking small house a little way down the road on the left hand side, at the end of a brief, stony track. A strand of telephone wire attached to the gable announced that it had a telephone, so the signs at this point were good. Soon I was tapping on the door and after a brief pause, I was looking into the cold stare of an elderly but unaccountably unwelcoming householder. I asked if I could make a couple of local telephone calls. We had broken down along the road a short distance away and I had to get the garage in Fort Augustus to give us a tow home. Silence greeted this very reasonable request. The chill stare was unblinking. I began to feel uncomfortable. Most people I had come in contact with up to that point in my life had been sort of reasonable in their responses to me. This was becoming decidedly odd. When he eventually spoke, it was to tell me that he was not happy about me using his phone. He did not know what it would cost to make the two calls and didn't know what to charge me. Now I was really getting nervous. I certainly couldn't afford to annoy him and have the door slammed on me.

"It shouldn't cost all that much," I said. "Just a couple of local calls."

He fixed me with his dull stare. "Well, how much do **you** think it would be?

This was becoming really ridiculous. What on earth was the matter with this oddity of nature who would seem to be denying even the basic social courtesies?

"Look. I've got my mother and grandmother in the car. I've got to get them home as soon as possible. Please let me use your phone. I'll pay you whatever you want. Surely that'll be all right?"

Another drawn-out pause. Then

"It'll cost half a crown then."

I was stunned. That was almost the equivalent of five pounds nowadays. But he was the man in charge and that was that. I reluctantly dug the large coin out of my pocket and handed it to him. He took it silently and indicated the phone on a small table by the window.

When I got back to the car I told the two anxious passengers of the incredible response to my appeal for help and the extortionate payment I had to make. Their reactions were predictable, but the problem now was the next stage. How long would the help from the garage take to arrive?

Fort Augustus had two garages in those days. Hughie Grant had the West End Garage, while his brother Ian had the one at our end of the village. Both had played shinty in the local team in their younger days. Apart from the fact that we dealt with Ian's garage, it was one eccentric feature of it that has left me with an indelible memory of the place. Whenever you passed it, either on foot on your bike, you knew that the proprietor was on the premises by the hollow, sepulchral coughing that followed each lungful of Capstan Full Strength he dragged down. It tore and echoed through the dark, oily depths of the building. Ian was an inveterate chain smoker. And here, I must be allowed a small diversion. When recently checking up on the phone some details of the background to all this story with my brother, he told me that shortly after he had moved down to work in Glasgow in the sixties, he was walking along Buchanan Street one Saturday. Suddenly, he heard a sound that immediately transported him back to his home village. It was a deep, dragging agonising cough. Surely not Ian Grant? People didn't travel so much in those days. But, sure enough, standing in a shop doorway and wearing the dark suit of the Highlander on holiday, was Ian with cigarette in hand and being racked by his habitual convulsions.

But to return to the business in hand. I can't remember the name of the Grant's Garage mechanic, but it was he, I was told over the phone, who would be setting off to rescue us with one of the garage lorries. He would tow us back to the village and the car would be seen to as soon as possible. I was already pretty nervous at the thought of being towed along the narrow swooping and twisting Garry road – something I had never experienced before. But being a garage, I also thought that Ian would have a vehicle adapted for the purpose. One of these breakdown ones with a sort of crane at the back maybe. So it would be all right, then?

I seem to remember that the first thought when the lorry did arrive was that it was pretty quick in getting to us. Certainly it was faster than I had imagined possible, knowing the distance. I heard it first. The frantic, raging engine note so familiar in those days of the popular Bedford petrol powered truck. Then I saw it against the darkening evening sky about a quarter of a mile away – bearing down on us. It had a sort of unsettling look about it. A wild sort of flapping in the wind. I stepped out to wave it down. It just swept past without a glance and disappeared into the distance. It was the Grant's Garage lorry without a doubt. I knew it well and the name and telephone number were there on the cab door. The engine note faded quickly in the distance. I was stunned. Surely he had seen us? The Riley was, so far as I knew, the only one in the Great Glen in those days and was highly distinctive. I had been standing right at the roadside waving. Morale was plunging. I was deeply unhappy. Far away, brake lights suddenly flared red. Something had clearly penetrated the consciousness of our rescuer and that he had just hurtled past the vehicle he had been sent to succour. There was a savage churning of gears as the Bedford was flung reversing up a road end and soon it was threshing its way back to our lay-by. It drew up in a spray of gravel and the mechanic leaped out, apologising cheerfully. Very cheerfully. Too cheerfully.

"Hope you've not been waiting too long," he said – directly into my face.

Now it was that the full awfulness of the situation struck me with force. The gust of breath that enveloped me in its clammy embrace was that of a man who was far from sober. He wasn't stumbling around or slurring his speech, but he had that watery-eyed garrulousness of the classic pub bore in full flow.

As I stood, gripped by indecision, he disappeared under the front of the Riley and began to tie a length of hairy rope to some projection he had found there. Then he tied the other end to something on the Bedford.

"OK. Now we're off. Remember to keep the towrope taut. If it goes slack, it'll snap when it takes the strain again. Keep using the brakes."

And this was the sum total of my instructions on what to do during the journey home with my silent, petrified passengers. This was truly an unfolding vision of hell.

The next hour or so of my life is compressed in my memory into a white-hot supernova of fear. From the moment the inebriated garage mechanic let in the clutch of the Bedford and the rope twanged rigid as it took the strain for the first time, I knew that we were plunging into a waking nightmare: a sweat-drenched crisis. I kept frantically pressing the footbrake to keep that wretched rope taut as instructed, but the erratic driving of the lorry made it impossible. We were swooping into one of the many dips in the road when I saw that the towrope was touching the road surface. The Bedford changed down noisily to tackle the hill approaching and, just as predicted, the rope snapped silently. Off he charged over the top of the hill and the engine note quickly faded in the distance. Rescue Man had not even noticed we were no longer there. Silence as we drifted to a halt. Again, the distant scream of tortured metal as reverse gear was engaged and there was the Bedford with its driver standing out on the running board, reversing at full tilt back to us. "Never noticed you'd gone," he announced breezily as he leaped down. Again the hasty scrabbling to re-attach us and he called out as he scrambled back into the cab, "You'll have to keep a closer eye on that bloody towrope!" Not much you can say to that.

Suffice to say that on the Garry road part of that dreadful journey, the abomination of a rope must have broken no fewer than ten times. I learned to leave the ignition switched on so that I could sound the hoarse blare of the Riley horn to attract Rescue Man's dulled attention on each occasion. Things were markedly better when we got to the main road because the gradients weren't so sudden – though the speed did increase alarmingly on occasion. Then, at last, the blessed towers of the Abbey ahead signalled the village and home and safety. Soon, we were drawing up on the forecourt of Grant's Garage. I was spent, totally and utterly. The passengers were mute. As we climbed slowly out of the Riley I became aware of a powerful, acrid smell that caught the throat. There seemed to be a haze – a sort of miasma hanging over the car. Ian's shout alerted us.

" Get clear of the car. Quick. The brakes look red hot. Get back!"

And we didn't stop to ask questions. The petrol tank was just short distance away from the shimmering brake drums. The brakes were indeed red hot as a result of constantly being applied for mile after relentless mile from away on far side of Invergarry. In fact, the whole system had to be repaired and all the brake pads replaced at no doubt appalling cost - though it's certain enough that the insurance would have helped.

But what no insurance policy on earth could ever have compensated for was the further driving into my mother's mind the conviction that motor travel was something unnatural for the human race and that she was going to convey that somehow to whoever was driving her to any destination in the future with even greater intensity.

Postscript

Ardvreck Publishing have asked me if this book was the sum total of my recollection of the Great Glen. Of course it isn't! Immediately, for starters, there springs to mind the dark image of the Fort Augustus Parish Priest, Father Philip, sitting glass in hand, in the old schoolhouse at the top of Bunoich Brae, where he was a regular visitor of my parents. He was a convivial man with a rich fund of tales. Ours was not a Roman Catholic house, so he may have felt less constrained among those out with the flock of Rome. It was his story about ghostly happenings on the road between Invermoriston and Inverness – and the manner of his telling – that stirred the imagination and sent delicious thrills along the spine. You were left with the thought *"Why would a priest invent something like that?"* After all, it is his calling to impart the concept of "ashes to ashes and dust to dust" and to dispel foolish notions like ghostly manifestations. Surely the events he described in that now long-vanished dining room must actually have taken place. It is not just the tale itself – intriguing and chilling as it is – but it is the extraordinary conclusion {if you can call it that} that it had about thirty years later in my own life.

September 2009

<u>Brian Denoon</u>